Happy birthd

Happy cooks
land of Oz

Hélène
12-26-90

TOUCHED
BY A
Rainbow

Text: Ron Welch

LEISURE
TIME
PUBLISHING
INC.
DALLAS, TX

Published by the Kansas State Board of Agriculture, Topeka, Kansas, in association with Leisure Time Publishing, a division of Heritage Worldwide, Inc., Dallas, Texas.

Publisher: Rodney L. Dockery
General Manager & Editorial Director: Caleb Pirtle III
Executive Editor: Ken Lively
Managing Editor: Sheri Harris

Regional Publishing Director: Suzanne Breitbach
Project Editor: Betty Miser
Food Editor: Diane Luther
Recipe Editor: Susan Lee
Art Director: Lynn Herndon Sullivan
Production Coordinator: Kathy Hazel
Production Manager: Vickie Craig

Photography provided by the Kansas Department of Commerce Travel and Tourism Division, the Kansas State Board of Agriculture, the Kansas Farm Bureau, The Kansas Farmer Magazine/HBJ Farm Publications and the Kansas Historical Society.

Cover Photograph: Dick Herpich, Lawrence, Kansas
Design: Jamie Pritchett

Recipes were provided by Kansas food manufacturers. However, in order to create a broader awareness of the many great products made in the state and to benefit you, the reader and cook, in your efforts to proudly support those products, Leisure Time Publishing has customized ingredients in the recipes with Kansas-made products.

Recipes in *Touched By A Rainbow* have been formatted for your convenience according to the *Handbook of Food Preparation,* developed by the American Home Economics Association.

First Printing

Manufactured in the United States of America

Printed by:
Heritage Worldwide, Inc.
9029 Directors Row
Dallas, Texas 75247
Telephone: (214) 630-4300

CONTENTS

ACKNOWLEDGEMENTS

The Kansas State Board of Agriculture Marketing Division appreciates the contribution of recipes from Kansas agricultural organizations and FROM THE LAND OF KANSAS companies. Traditional family to haute cuisine recipes, reflect the state's finest foods. In Kansas, travel and food are natural partners whether traveling to see friends or visiting one of the state's many tourist attractions.

Kansas State Board of Agriculture
Eldon Fastrup, Marketing Division Director
Charlene Patton
Rodney Ferguson
Hayley Matson
Teresa Booher

Associated Milk Producers, Inc.
Dairy Council, Inc.
Kansas Association of Wheat Growers
Kansas Beef Council
Kansas Commercial Fish Growers Association
Kansas Corn Growers Association
Kansas Honey Producers Association
Kansas Pork Producers Council
Kansas Poultry Association
Kansas Sheep Association
Kansas Soybean Association
Kansas Wheat Commission

Alma Manor

Special assistance provided by:
Kansas Department of Commerce, Travel and Tourism Division

FOREWORD

Kansas has long had a proud agricultural heritage. Its farmers, its ranchers, its food manufacturers and processors literally feed the world.

And the Kansas State Board of Agriculture, through the years, has developed one of the most effective, most respected programs in the nation to market Kansas foods from one corner of the country to the other.

FROM THE LAND OF KANSAS is its trademark.

Now, from the land of Kansas comes *Touched By A Rainbow,* a totally new concept that captures the flavor, the spirit, the essence of Kansas in an innovative travel cookbook.

Produced jointly by the Kansas State Board of Agriculture and Leisure Time Publishing, *Touched By A Rainbow: Great Cooking From The Land of Kansas* is filled with Kansas-styled recipes that showcase Kansas-made products.

In addition, it provides editorial narrative on scenic, historic and recreational Kansas, ably penned by Ron Welch, one of the state's most noted and widely-read travel writers.

Touched By A Rainbow proudly becomes part of the Kansas State Board of Agriculture's year-round "Celebrate! Kansas Food" retail promotion, developed to assist some 300 companies which presently participate in the statewide program. There are also radio and television programs, advertising campaigns, grocery store promotions, brochures, catalogs, and participation in national trade shows and food fairs.

But then, FROM THE LAND OF KANSAS has one vital goal—to enhance the sale of Kansas products.

And why not?

Statewide surveys have proven that eighty-eight percent of all consumers within the state prefer to buy Kansas products, and ninety-two percent of them immediately recognize, understand, and appreciate the benefits of the Kansas trademark.

Touched By A Rainbow simply gives you more than two hundred new reasons—with more than two hundred recipes—to use Kansas products every time you go to the kitchen to prepare a family meal.

That's good for the state.

That's good for Kansas farmers, ranchers and food manufacturers.

And, just as importantly, it's good for you and your family.

INTRODUCTION

M y parents' announcement that we would be moving to Kansas was acknowledged, nonchalantly, by my brothers and me. You adopt that attitude when your father is a military officer who is transferred regularly.

Dad was a navigator-bombardier on B-47s and his new duty station was Wichita's McConnell Air Force Base. We moved into a house in the small town of Mulvane, ten miles south of the base. We saw something in that community we liked . . . a down home friendliness . . that is pervasive across Kansas today. They still live in that house, in retirement.

My folks had developed a love affair with Kansas, something my brothers and I have come to appreciate now that we're in our 40s. Our own military services took us to bases in such desirable Sun Belt cities as San Antonio, Phoenix and Tucson. Yet, after spending enjoyable times there, Kansas drew us back.

I've never lost my affection for Kansas, even though I've traveled to forty-nine states (I'll get to you someday, Delaware) and abroad. What we have here isn't the fantasy world of Disney, or the carnival-like atmosphere of Branson, Gatlinburg and Coney Island. Most of our major attractions are based on real people and events.

My extensive travels throughout Kansas, for the last twenty-five or so years, have taken me to nearly every city and town in the state, past and present. I've seen where aviatrix Amelia Earhart grew up in Atchison; a small museum in Sedan that keeps alive the memory of Emmett Kelly, a local boy who became the most famous circus clown ever; and the Abilene boyhood home of Dwight D. Eisenhower.

I've visited towns like Buttermilk, Gas and Gem; learned that Havana is closer to Peru than it is to Cuba; and stopped in Minneapolis, Manhattan and Erie without ever having left the state.

Then I've had the good fortune to meet many Kansans themselves . . . native sons and daughters, and transplants like me. People like:

Carl Storey, and his wife, Fern, who taught me what real work was, stacking hay on a trailer behind a baler and in barns.

And, the late Alf Landon, centenarian, former presidential candidate, and outspoken politician who said, "There are some intelligent people in Washington. More of 'em in Kansas."

Since this book also relates to cooking I've mentioned some of the Kansas restaurants I've come across in my travels, ones that locals eat at. Many are easy to find like Salina's Cozy Inn. Others require directions. If you're in Topeka, for example, you'll never find Don's Steak House or the Topeka Steak House without asking. The same goes for Guy & Mae's in Williamsburg, truly off the beaten path.

You'll learn many things about Kansas' five tourism regions in the following text but the best way to know the state is to travel its highways and byways as I do. Enjoy the natural and man-made attractions. Sample the good food we have to offer. Meet the people. You'll find that one of God's treasures "Touched By A Rainbow," is Kansas.

SOUTHWEST KANSAS

Cattle is king in Southwest Kansas, as it has been for more than a century. Cowboys still round up livestock but mostly from large feedlots, not the open range. And, instead of loading the animals onto railroad freight cars bound for meatpackers in Chicago, they're shipped by trucks to huge processing plants in Dodge City, Holcomb and Liberal.

How large are the feedlots?

They're so large that tourists often stop in awe to take pictures of them. At one, just outside Dodge City, a scenic overlook was constructed next to Highway 50 to prevent vehicle accidents.

Southwest Kansas is also Wild West history. The Dalton Gang, Bat Masterson and Wyatt Earp were some of the most famous characters from its past. The Long Branch Saloon and Front Street were legends in their own time, remembered today through interpretive programs at Dodge City's Boot Hill Museum.

Dodge City is one of the most famous of towns in the early West. It was founded in 1872 as a supply center for buffalo hunters.

Front Street is a reconstruction of two blocks of the original 1878 business district of Dodge City. Its exhibits range from the Bank of Dodge City, to the Rice Brothers' saddle shop, to the home of Squirrel Tooth Alice, a "lady of the evening." They were called "soiled doves" back then.

There is also the Rath and Wright General Store, the old Fort Dodge Jail, John Tyler's Tonsorial Parlor, The Saratoga Saloon and Beatty & Kelley's Dodge City Restaurant. The Beeson Museum includes replicas of the marshal's office and several businesses. An extensive firearms collection features Sharps, Springfield, Colt, Remington and Winchester rifles and pistols.

Other exhibits include a 1917 one-room schoolhouse, a Santa Fe Railway depot complete with a 1903 locomotive, an 1880 carriage shed and the 1878 home of R.J. Hardesty. Hardesty was a cattle rancher whose family resided in the structure until 1914.

Boot Hill Museum is located on the original site of the cemetery bearing the same name. It presents the story of what was once labeled the "Wickedest Little City in America."

Yes, "Miss Kitty" kicks up her heels along with other cancan dancers at the Long Branch Variety Show. Accompanied by "Doc" at the piano, she sings and dances.

"Cattle, Wheat & Storekeepers," presented at the museum, documents the city's economic growth during the cattle drive era. For a decade, more than ten million Texas longhorns were brought up the Chisholm and Western trails to the Santa Fe Railway loading pens in Dodge City. As the town grew, the Wild West slowly disappeared and the lands surrounding it were converted to crop raising and cattle grazing.

Popular entertainment at the Boot Hill Museum complex during summer months includes tours of the grounds aboard the Boot Hill Stage Line, gunfights (blanks only!), melodramas and medicine shows. A favorite entertainment is the evening western chuckwagon dinner which includes Kansas beef, cooked to perfection, plus beans, cole slaw and other side dishes. Extra to the Boot Hill Museum admission, but well worth it.

Five miles east of Dodge City is Fort Dodge. Once a supply depot and base of operations against the Indians, it is now a veterans home.

Nine miles west of the Cowboy Capital is a small park where ruts left by the passage of wagon trains over the Santa Fe Trail can still be seen.

Other must-see stops in Dodge City include Cowboy Statue and Yoked Oxen Monument.

"Gunsmoke" fans will want to visit Saint Mary of the Plains college. Much of the memorabilia "Doc" (actor Milburn Stone, a native of Burrton, Kansas) left to the school is on exhibit.

The Dodge City, Ford & Bucklin Railroad runs passenger excursions year-round. A vintage steam locomotive pulls two passenger cars and a caboose from the station at Water Sports Campground in South Dodge (go south on Second Street to Sycamore, then head east) on a one and a half hour trip to Wilroads Gardens and back. Concessions, souvenirs and a restroom are on board.

Dodge City Days, in August, is the city's major celebration. Champion cowboys and cowgirls from the Professional Rodeo Cowboy's Association display their talents at Dodge City Days, before performing in the famous Cheyenne Frontier Days in Cheyenne, Wyoming and the Calgary Stampede in Calgary, Alberta Canada.

The streets of Sitka, Kansas (population 2), aren't "rolled up at 5 p.m.," as the popular adage goes, because there aren't any. Besides, there's more nightlife in the Clark County community than meets the eye.

Buddy and Kathy Probst operate the Old Weigh Station and Sitka Social Club. They open at 6 a.m. and close "whenever we feel like it," says Kathy, "but sometimes not until the wee hours."

Dress, as might be expected, is casual.

"But don't wear your hat inside unless you want the bartender to add it to her collection," Kathy warns.

If you're a first timer to the Old Weigh Station and are not familiar with the menu, look at the chalkboard—it's there. It'll still be the same the next time you visit, except for the daily special.

The best chicken fried steak I've ever eaten (heavier on the pepper than most) and hamburger steak are popular items. All meat is fresh. The french fries still have their skins. And, because "the bread company won't deliver out here," Kathy says, "Buddy and Starla Cook bake all of the breads and pies."

Tables are made by a local craftsman. Decorations include a wall in the club that displays the brands of local ranchers who brought their branding irons in one night for a "burn".

The Probsts' original Sitka restaurant was in an old house that once served as a weigh station.

"Truckers would stop in all the time and bring their papers," Kathy relates. "They thought we were still a weigh station."

Tragically, fire destroyed the building.

"Buddy and I didn't want to give up though, so we temporarily opened a ten-stool diner in a Valentine trailer that had been all over the country."

Local folks got to hankerin' for a more permanent, full-service, restaurant so the Probsts' bought an old schoolhouse from the state and moved it across the road.

"People around here donated what we have on the walls," Kathy proudly notes. "Implements, signs, etcetera. They even brought in tables and chairs so we could open."

APPETIZERS

After a long ride, Barber County

Photo by George Smith

7

To show their appreciation, Buddy and Kathy held a huge covered dish picnic each Memorial Day for several years. They furnished hamburgers, buns and pop. Now they serve breakfast following the Easter sunrise services on nearby Mt. Jesus.

Sitka is hard to find, so here's how to get there. Look on a Kansas map for the communities of Ashland and Protection. Sitka is located between them, just south of the U.S. Highways 160, 183 and K-34.

The buffalo still roam on the other side of Clark County from Sitka. They are in the Big Basin and St. Jacob's Well areas.

St. Jacob's Well is a beautiful spot, sixteen miles west of Ashland. Legend says the well has no bottom. Certainly it has never run dry. The natural well was a popular watering hole during the cattle drive era, frequented by cowboys headed from Texas to Dodge City.

The Pioneer Museum in Ashland is interesting not only for its collection of items from days past, but because of Harold Krier's memorabilia. The late world champion aerobatic pilot donated three of his planes, trophies and awards to the small attraction.

Hardesty House, on Ashland's Main Street, is a small hotel featuring turn-of-the-century furniture and decor. Rooms with antique furniture and private baths are available for rent.

Proprietors Richard and Tracy Thorne also operate one of the leading places to eat in Kansas. Their Sunday buffet is well patronized. Prime rib is a specialty of the house.

The outcome of one of the world's most unusual races is decided every Shrove Tuesday, the day before Ash Wednesday, in Liberal, Kansas.

Although fifteen contestants can complete, each runner might have

Bean Dip with Deep-Fried Pasta

1 (16 oz) can refried beans

1 cup shredded Alma Cheddar Cheese

2 tbsp Rabbit Creek Spicey Mexican Dip Mix

- Combine refried beans, cheese and dip mix.
- Cook over medium heat or in microwave until cheese is melted.
- Place in serving bowl.
- Serve hot or cold.
- Makes 2 cups.

Deep-Fried Pasta:

1 box rotelle or bow pasta

salad oil for deep frying

1 tsp Carey Salt

- Cook pasta according to pkg directions.
- Drain well and rinse with cold water.
- Let stand until pasta is almost dry and sticky before frying.
- Meanwhile, heat 1″ oil in deep-fat fryer or large pan to 375 degrees.
- With slotted spoon, transfer pasta, 1 cup at a time, into the oil.
- Fry, 3-5 minutes, until crisp and golden brown. Drain on paper towels. Sprinkle with salt.
- Serve with dip.

7 Layer Dip

1 (16 oz) can refried beans

1 cup guacamole

1 cup sour cream

1 cup shredded lettuce

1 cup shredded Alma Cheddar Cheese

1 cup chopped tomatoes

½ cup chopped black olives

½ cup Fuego Picante Sauce

Spanish Gardens Tortilla Chips

- Layer each of the ingredients in the order given, except picante sauce and chips.
- Spread each layer ½″ thick.
- Just before serving, drizzle picante sauce over the top.
- Serve immediately with crisp tortilla chips.
- Serves 20-25.

another fifteen "unseen" opponents she must outdistance to be declared champion. A first-place finish in the annual Sunflower State event doesn't guarantee a victory. It could mean the winner is runner-up instead. To complicate matters, a good long distance telephone connection is necessary to verify the race's final results.

Shrove Tuesday is better known in Liberal, and Olney, England, as International Pancake Day. The highlight of the festivities features housewives in the two communities sprinting a four hundred fifteen-yard "S" shaped course, clad in traditional garb, an apron and headscarf. Further, each contestant is obligated to carry a skillet with a pancake in it. The flapjack must be flipped immediately after the race begins and as soon as the runner crosses the finish line. Winning times in each city are then compared, via transatlantic telephone, to determine whether the Americans or English have captured the championship.

The international competition, begun in 1950, is relatively new in the race's history. Legend has it that Olney's first "runner" completed the British course more than five hundred years ago.

English housewives of that period customarily used up accumulated cooking fats by baking pancakes the day before Lenten fasting began, or Shrove Tuesday. One Olney woman became so involved with her baking that she lost track of the time until the church bells rang, calling everyone to shriving service. Not wanting to be late, she forgot to remove her apron and, skillet in hand, dashed to Olney's church. Amused neighbors decided to make the run an annual contest to see which housewife could reach the church steps first, from a common starting place. Since then, the winner has received a kiss from the local verger (bell ringer) with the words, "The peace of the Lord always be with you."

American involvement in the competition occurred by accident. Rodney J. Leete, a former vice president of the Liberal Jaycee chapter, was browsing through a national magazine when he saw a picture of Olney's race. He cabled Ronald Collins, vicar of the English village, challenging the housewives of Olney to compete against their Liberal counterparts. Collins readily accepted. Annually, since that time, the

Fiesta Beef Dip

1 lb ground beef

1 medium onion, chopped

1 (6 oz) can tomato paste

1 (8 oz) can tomato sauce

1½ cups shredded American cheese

1 cup shredded Pioneer Cheddar Cheese

1 (4 oz) can chopped green chilies, drained

Tostitos® Chips

- Cook ground beef and onion until meat is browned; drain.
- Blend in remaining ingredients and heat until cheese melts.
- Serve warm with chips.
- Makes 4 cups.

Beer Cheese Dip

1 (16 oz) pkg processed cheese spread, softened

1 (8 oz) pkg cream cheese, softened

2 tbsp Rabbit Creek Country Herb Dip Mix

¾ cup beer

assorted crackers

- Combine and heat cheese spread, cream cheese, dip mix and beer.
- Add more beer if a thinner consistency is desired.
- When thoroughly heated, serve with crackers.
- Makes 3 cups.

Jo's Dip

1 (8 oz) pkg cream cheese

1 cup sour cream

2 tsp Ken's Blend Chili Seasoning

chips or fresh vegetables

- Whip or blend ingredients together until smooth.
- Dip with chips or fresh vegetables.
- Makes 2 cups.

contest has been held in the spirit of goodwill and friendship.

The starter's gun is fired at 11:55 a.m. in each country. The time difference between the two means the English portion of the race is completed several hours before Liberal's is staged. Modern technology has made the transatlantic telephone call comparing times merely a formal courtesy for the Americans. Satellites permit the American media to find out Olney's results before the Kansas runners begin, and invariably that information is leaked.

Liberal's first victory came in 1952. Since then the advantage has shifted between the cities with Olney now holding a slight edge.

The race's only "no contest" was declared in 1980 because of an incident in England. A British Broadcasting Corporation (BBC) truck used to televise the event inadvertently blocked the course and the runners there were unable to complete it.

What began as a modest effort for fun once a year has blossomed into a four-day event. No longer limited to just a race and pancake feed, Liberal's biggest celebration includes a parade, talent shows, concerts, eating contests and the traditional worship service.

The pancake eating contests for men, women and children are tests of strategy as well as gluttony. Some participants take each of their regulation-size flapjacks and squeeze them into a ball before consuming them. The object is to get all of the air out. Others sip liquids only at predetermined intervals in their quest. Adult winners usually eat more than fifty pancakes in a single sitting.

Shrove Tuesday in Liberal, begins with a pancake breakfast at the National Guard Armory. Local civic club members and other volunteers are lined up at grills flipping flapjacks to serve the hundreds of people attending the all-you-can-eat meal. The modest sum charged also buys juice, coffee and sausage, served in limited portions.

Children's races start at 10 a.m. Events are held, on a shortened course, for toddlers through junior high school age — females only!

Males aren't totally excluded from competition. A men's pacer race sets the stage for the women's main event. Like the women, they must

Southwestern Cheesecake

1 cup finely crushed La Siesta
Tortilla Chips

3 tbsp melted margarine

2 (8 oz) pkgs cream cheese, softened

2 eggs

1 (8 oz) pkg Alma Colby or Monterey
Jack Cheese, shredded

1 (4 oz) can chopped green chilies,
drained

1 cup sour cream

1 cup chopped yellow or orange
bell pepper

½ cup green onion slices

⅓ cup Harvest House tomatoes

¼ cup pitted ripe olive slices

- Combine chips and margarine; press onto bottom of 9″ springform pan.
- Bake in 325 degree oven for 15 minutes.
- Beat cream cheese and eggs at medium speed until well blended.
- Mix in shredded cheese and chilies and pour over crust.
- Bake 30 minutes.
- Spread sour cream over cheesecake.
- Loosen cake from rim of pan and cool before removing rim.
- Chill.
- Top with remaining ingredients just before serving.
- Makes 16-20 servings.

Cherry Tomatoes with Herb Filling

30 firm Organic Country
Table Cherry Tomatoes

1 (8 oz) pkg cream cheese, softened

½ cup sour cream

2 tbsp Rabbit Creek Country
Herb Dip Mix

lettuce leaves

- Wash and dry cherry tomatoes, and remove any stems.
- With a sharp serrated knife, cut off the round bottom of each tomato, remove the seeds and pulp with a small melon-ball scoop, and put the tomatoes, cut-side down, on paper towels or a wire rack to drain.
- Refrigerate until ready to fill.
- To make filling, combine the cream cheese, sour cream and dip mix.
- Use a small spoon to fill the tomatoes with the mixture, and place the tomatoes on a bed of lettuce leaves, which will keep the tomatoes from rolling.
- Makes 30 servings.

Historic Dodge City, Ford County

Cheese Spread

7 oz Gouda or Edam cheese
2 tbsp cream cheese
2 tbsp Fuego Salsa
1 green onion, chopped (optional)
1-2 tbsp chopped jalapeno peppers (optional)
Santa Fe Tortilla Chips

- Beat cheese, cream cheese, salsa, green onion and jalapeno peppers until blended.
- Chill several hours or overnight.
- Let stand at room temperature before serving.
- Serve with tortilla chips.
- Makes 1 cup.

Harvest Cheese Ball

1 (8 oz) pkg cream cheese
1 (8 oz) pkg Neufchatel cheese
1 (8 oz) pkg shredded Cheddar cheese
1½ cups Kansas Wheat House Cracked Wheat
1 tsp liquid smoke
¼ cup chopped onions
3 oz Kansas Wheat House Wheat Nubs

- Mix the cheeses in a food processor or by hand.
- Add the cracked wheat, liquid smoke and chopped onions.
- Blend all together.
- Roll into 3 large balls, and dip balls into wheat nubs.
- Keep in refrigerator until ready to eat.

Jalapeno-Pepper Jelly Appetizer

1 (8 oz) pkg cream cheese
1 cup Chautauqua Hills Jalapeno-Pepper Jelly
assorted crackers

- Spread a brick of cream cheese with jalapeno-pepper jelly.
- Serve with crackers.
- Serves 10-12.

run four hundred fifteen-yards. Although they, too, must wear aprons and headscarfs, dresses give way to running shorts.

In contrast to the hoopla surrounding Liberal's event, Olney's continues to be low key. Schools aren't closed for the day, there are no parades, however, enthusiasm for the contest runs high. But more important than the spirit of competition between Liberal and Olney, is the bond of friendship the two cities have shared for years.

W hile attending an insurance convention in California, Max Zimmerman's Liberal lapel pin was noticed by another participant. "I've always wanted to go to Kansas, to see Dorothy's house," the man commented.

Though the exact location where Dorothy began her famous flight in the "Wizard of Oz" has never been established, Zimmerman wondered later, "Why not Liberal?" He presented his idea to the local Seward County Historical Society, which adopted the plan. Society president, Oliver S. Brown, then began efforts to recreate Oz.

Brown's first challenge was to find a suitable structure for remodeling into a replica of the frame farmhouse in which Dorothy lived with her Uncle Henry, Aunt Em, and dog, Toto.

"We sent to MGM (Metro Goldwyn Mayer) studios for a set of plans that detailed the house's shape, contents and other pertinent information," Brown recalled. "They were kind enough to give us everything we wanted, right down to pictures to hang on the walls."

Brown then set off to find a building. He located exactly what he was looking for on the Robert Rice farm. The Rice family believed the project had merit and donated their abandoned pioneer dwelling to the historical society.

Liberal's Raymond Hubbard refurbished the house to duplicate Dorothy's, complete with items typical of the 1907-1909 period when Frank Baum wrote the Oz story.

Little Cheddar Sausage Biscuits

1 cup HearTland Mill® Unbleached Flour
1 cup HearTland Mill® Whole Wheat Flour
2 tsp baking powder
½ tsp baking soda
6 tbsp butter
1½ cups shredded Cheddar cheese
¾ cup buttermilk
2 lbs Lone Pine Farms Sausage

- Mix together dry ingredients.
- Cut in butter and cheese; blend well.
- Stir in buttermilk and mix to form a soft dough.
- Knead 20-25 times. Roll out to ½" thickness.
- Cut into 2" biscuits.
- Bake in 450 degree oven for 10-12 minutes.
- Meanwhile, fry 2" sausage patties.
- Slice biscuits in half horizontally and fill with sausage patty.
- Makes 2 doz.

Ham Balls

2 lbs Galey's Smoked Ground Ham
2 lbs fresh ground pork
½ cup finely ground Rainbo Bread
1 tbsp celery flakes
½ cup minced onion
2 tbsp garlic salt

- Mix all ingredients well; shape into balls.
- Bake in shallow pan in 350 degree oven for 30 minutes.
- Serve hot.
- Makes 48 balls.

Sausage Balls

1 lb Lone Pine Farms Sausage
1 cup shredded Cheddar cheese
1 cup HearTland Mill® Buttermilk Quick Mix

- Mix all ingredients together; form into small balls.
- Bake in 425 degree oven until browned.
- Makes 24 balls.

Brown offered an interesting side note to Baum's saga.

"Baum had a hard time selling his book. Although the story was based on an actual Kansas family, in a real Kansas farmhouse, his fictionalizing was too far-fetched for some editors."

Of course Dorothy's House wouldn't be complete without a yellow brick road. It winds from the front door of the home over a bridge to the Coronado Historical Museum.

In addition to seeing Dorothy's House and bona fide furnishings, visitors to the attraction are treated to a fifteen-minute film clip featuring actual footage from the beginning and ending of the classic motion picture.

While at Dorothy's House, spend some time at the Coronado Historical Museum. It contains relics and exhibits related to the famous Spanish explorer Francisco Vasquez de Coronado who marched north from Mexico in 1540, through much of southwestern and south central Kansas, in search of the fabled "Seven Golden Cities of Cibola." A bronze statue of the conquistador, on museum grounds, commemorates his exploits.

K ansas' largest aviation museum is also in Liberal. It prides itself in displaying an outstanding collection of military and civilian aircraft plus aerospace aviation artifacts.

Among the Liberal Air Museum's vintage aircraft is a Grumman TBM Avenger, the U.S. Navy's heavy-duty torpedo bomber utilized during World War II. Also, a Douglas A-4 Skyhawk, a light-weight fighter with a knock-out punch; a Vought F8U-2N Crusader, a Mach 1.97 aircraft carrier-borne fighter which saw extensive action in the Vietnam conflict; a North American B-25, the "Iron Laiden Maiden" that was one of America's World War II mainstays in the Pacific theater; and a Rutan Aircraft with a unique "tail first" design by the creator of the famous around-the-world aircraft, "Voyager." More than fifty other aircraft are

Barbecue Meatballs

¾ cup evaporated milk
1½ lbs Blazek Ground Beef
1 cup rolled oats
1 egg
½ cup chopped onion
½ tsp garlic powder
1 tsp Pedro Lopez Chili Powder
¼ tsp Carey Salt
1 (20 oz) btl Curley's Hickory Barbecue Sauce

- Mix all ingredients except sauce; shape into a ball the size of a walnut, or smaller if used as an appetizer.
- Make ahead of time, and refrigerate, if possible, to enhance flavor.
- Place on cookie sheet in a single layer.
- Cover generously with sauce and bake in 350 degree oven for 35-45 minutes.
- After baking, place in slow cooker on low heat and pour on more sauce.
- Simmer and serve.
- Makes 24 meatballs.

Bob's B-Q Chicken Wings

2 lbs chicken wings
1 (18 oz) btl Bob's B-Q Sauce
beer or light wine (optional)

- Cut chicken wings at joint and discard tips.
- Brown in skillet or hot oven until browned. Drain on paper towel.
- Place chicken wings in shallow baking dish or casserole in single layer.
- Cover with sauce to coat. Put into 350 degree oven for 20 minutes, turning to coat after 10 minutes.
- If sauce becomes too thick, thin with beer or wine.
- Use extra sauce for dipping.
- Serves 10-12.

in the collection.

Located at the Liberal Municipal Airport, the museum was established to help preserve America's proud aviation history.

Eva Dalton had a little shop in Meade, Kansas, where she made and sold ladies' hats and "finery." She also had some brothers who preferred robbery to working.

Emmett Dalton showed up in Meade for Eva's wedding to J. N. Whipple who was described as a "half-hearted merchant and a whole-hearted poker player." Emmett soon visited the couple in their honeymoon house south of town and liked it . . . for a hideout.

Other brothers joined Emmett in paying regular visits to the Whipples in the years that followed.

Often those visits came shortly before or after horses were stolen and trains were robbed as far as forty miles away.

Rumor had it that Eva condoned, if not participated in, her brothers' activities. Uncomfortable with the local gossip, the Whipples abandoned their home in 1893 and slipped quietly out of Meade County.

The new owners, who bought the house at a tax sale, found strangers frequently tying their horses in the barn. The riders always seemed to arrive hastily and scurry for cover.

Investigation led to discovery of a tunnel, covered with boards and dirt, leading from a passage under the stairway of the house to the barn. It was ninety-five-feet long, proof that the Daltons could work when they had to.

Today the Whipple home is restored as it was in 1887 and the tunnel has been reconstructed to make it possible for the average-sized visitor to walk the Dalton's escape route to the barn.

A museum in the barn, immortalizing The Dalton Gang Hideout, contains items from pioneer days, including the W.S. Dingess antique gun collection, one of the finest in the nation.

Cocktail Buffalo Meat Balls in Tomato-Wine Sauce

1 lb Butterfield's Buffalo Burger

¾ lb pork, finely ground

1 small onion

1 small clove garlic, minced

1 egg

1 tsp finely chopped parsley

1 tsp lemon juice

1 tbsp Worcestershire sauce

1 cube chicken bouillon

¼ tsp salt

1 cup water

2 tbsp tomato puree

1 cup olive oil

1 cup Balkan Winery White Wine

- Combine buffalo, pork, onion, garlic, egg, lemon juice, Worcestershire sauce, parsley and salt.

- Knead the mixture well; roll into small meat balls.

- Heat olive oil over medium heat until very hot; fry meat balls until brown on all sides.

- In sauce pan over low heat dissolve bouillon in water. Slowly add tomato puree and wine. Let mixture come to a boil. Pour over meat balls, cover and simmer 15 minutes.

- Serve in chafing dish.

- Makes 3 doz appetizers.

Super Bowl With Dippers

11 strips Fanestil's Thick Sliced Bluestem Bacon, divided

2 (8 oz) pkgs cream cheese, at room temperature

¼ cup milk

¼ cup instant minced onion

¼ cup chopped green pepper

¼ tsp black pepper

1 cup sour cream

1 loaf (1 lb), 8" round sour dough bread

assorted Swift Premium Cold Cuts, broccoli flowerets, cauliflower flowerets, carrot sticks, cherry tomatoes, with stems

- Fry bacon until crisp. Drain. Chop fine. Reserve 1 tbsp for garnish.

- Blend cream cheese and milk in small bowl with electric mixer.

- Add bacon except reserved tbsp.

- Add seasonings and sour cream to cream cheese-bacon mixture. Blend thoroughly.

- Cut off top of loaf. Hollow out inside leaving ¼" thick walls and bottom. Fill with dip. Replace top.

- Wrap in foil and bake at 300 degrees for 1½ hours.

- Remove foil and top of bread. Sprinkle dip with reserved bacon.

- Arrange bread bowl on serving tray with the rolled cold cuts and fresh vegetables to use as dippers.

- Serves 16-20.

Kathleen Holt jokingly refers to her Cimarron Hotel as the booby prize from her divorce. The Holts had planned to operate a hotel and restaurant together, but she was the only one to stick around until the job was done.

"It took a lot of work to get it open and it requires a lot of work to keep it open," she emphasizes.

Holt's hotel, sixteen miles west of Dodge City, is well-known for its family-style Sunday dinners of pan-fried chicken and tender roast beef (plus creamy cole slaw or chunky applesauce, mashed potatoes and gravy, seasoned green beans, biscuits and honey, butter, homemade gingerbread and beverages). It is also a popular gathering place for amateur sleuths anxious to test their skill at the detective game.

A cast of local characters mingle with hotel guests to weave a complicated plot which involves everyone on the hotel register. The role playing is convincing. Fact and fiction seem inseparable. And in the end, those with the prowess to crack the case become the whodunit hero.

Local tongue-in-cheek legend has it that Cimarron received its name from pioneers, who, stopping to camp in the area before crossing the Arkansas River, put beans on to boil for their supper. When evening came and the beans still were not done, they were left to cook overnight. Morning arrived, and the beans were still not tender. The pioneers packed up their wagons, crossed the river, and left the beans to "simmer on."

The Cimarron Hotel was built by Nichola B. Klaine, editor and publisher of the Dodge City Times, in 1886. Three years later, during a county seat fight, local men used the cupola atop the three-story structure to watch for men from nearby Ingalls. Cimarron won, however, and the cupola has long since been removed.

At one time the hotel had seven competitors locally, now there are

BREADS

Medicine Lodge in the Gypsum Hills

Photo by Loreen Locke McMillan

none. Although the rooms are not furnished as they originally were, Holt has done much to preserve the history and charm of her place. Bathrooms are down the hall. And there are no telephones or television sets in the rooms either.

"Guests can enjoy the creaking of the oak floors, the high ceilings and the original wainscoting," Holt says. "The town is safe to stroll at night, we have a big front porch, and Clark's Pharmacy, down the street has an old-fashioned soda fountain."

Holt's restaurant features original tin ceilings as well as period pieces such as an ornate floor-to-ceiling mirror which was originally in the Mississippi governor's mansion.

G arden City celebrates Beef Empire Days in June, which hints to what the local economy is tied. If you want a good steak, head to Garden City.

And the best of the best? My favorite is the Grain Bin restaurant at the Wheatlands Motor Inn.

Finnup Park, in Garden City, has quite an outdoor swimming pool. It's half a city block in size and contains two and one-half million gallons of water. Although there is a large crew of full-time lifeguards, everyone swims for free.

The Lee Richardson Zoo, also in the park, contains nearly seven hundred mammals and birds in its forty-seven acres. That's a pretty good size for a community with a population under 20,000.

Zoo species range from an African elephant to animals of the South American pampas. A unique feature of the facility is that cars are allowed to drive within it. There are also shady pathways for walkers.

Garden City is a major retail center for Southwest Kansas. It has a vibrant downtown area.

Garden City's historical Windsor Hotel, built in 1886, was known as "The Waldorf of the Prairies." Although it is closed now, Buffalo Bill

Zucchini'N Cheese Corn Bread

1½ cups HearTland Mill® Unbleached
White Flour

¾ cup HearTland Mill® Corn Meal

2 tbsp sugar

4 tsp baking powder

1¼ tsp salt

1 cup milk

1 cup coarsely shredded Bismarck
Gardens Zucchini

1 cup shredded Cheddar cheese

1½ cups chopped green onion

¼ cup vegetable oil

2 Sunnyfresh Farms Eggs, beaten

- Preheat oven to 400 degrees.
- Grease 9″ square baking dish.
- Combine all dry ingredients.
- Add remaining ingredients, mixing just until dry ingredients are moistened.
- Pour into prepared pan.
- Bake 30 minutes or until golden brown.
- Serves 6-8.

Apple Cheddar Nut Bread

3 cups Lormak Farms Mills
Biscuit Mix

¼ cup sugar

½ tsp cinnamon

1 egg

½ cup milk

2 cups peeled, chopped Valley
Pride Apples

¾ cup chopped nuts

1 cup shredded Alma Sharp
Cheddar Cheese

- Combine biscuit mix, sugar, cinnamon, egg and milk.
- Stir vigorously for 30 seconds.
- Stir in apples, nuts and cheese.
- Pour into greased 9″ x 5″ loaf pan.
- Bake in 350 degree oven for 55-60 minutes.
- Cool before slicing.
- Makes 1 loaf.

100% Whole Wheat Bread

1 cup warm milk

2 pkgs active dry yeast

1 cup warm water, 90 degrees

⅓ cup Sweetheart Honey

6-7 cups Groth Farms Whole Wheat Flour, divided

2 eggs

2 tsp salt

¼ cup shortening

- Scald milk and cool.
- Dissolve yeast in warm water in large mixing bowl; add milk and honey.
- Beat in 3 cups flour and eggs.
- Beat 100 strokes or 2-3 minutes on medium mixer speed.
- Cover bowl and let stand 20-30 minutes.
- Mix in salt and remaining flour, ½ cup at a time, until dough can be turned out on a lightly floured surface to knead.
- If using dough hook, add shortening and complete by kneading on dough hook 8 minutes.
- If kneading by hand, knead 10-15 minutes, gradually kneading in shortening.
- Let dough rise in greased and covered bowl until doubled.
- Punch dough and divide in half.
- Let dough stand while greasing 2, 8″ x 4″ dough bread pans.
- Shape, place in pans, and let rise until doubled.
- Bake in 375 degree oven 8-10 minutes; then at 350 degrees for 10-20 minutes.
- Makes 2 loaves.

Cody, Eddie Foy and Lillian Russell were among the celebrities who stayed there.

South of the city is the Finney County Wildlife Area, a three thousand acre preserve with a herd of more than fifty buffalo. The refuge also supports deer, rabbits, coyotes, foxes, badgers, pheasant, quail, and other prairie animals.

El Quartelejo, north of Scott City, is the northernmost Indian pueblo in the Americas. Located in Scott County State Park, it was occupied by the Taos and Picurie Indians from 1650 to 1720.

This National Historic Monument is an important archaeological site. It is believed that the Indian inhabitants escaped Spanish oppression in what is now New Mexico and settled there.

The terrain in Scott County State Park is rugged and picturesque with deep canyons and craggy bluffs. It is also a popular vacation retreat, having a swimming beach at the state lake.

Near the park is Squaw's Den Battleground where the last Indian battle in Kansas occurred between the Northern Cheyenne nation and the U.S. Cavalry.

Monument Rocks are approximately ten miles to the north and east of the park.

Give Hamilton County residents a foot or two of water in the Arkansas River bed and they act like Californians when the surf's up. Amidst a party atmosphere, huge livestock tanks are loaded onto pickups and trailers, coolers are iced, and a caravan heads for the "beach" west of Syracuse.

"Tankin'" provides water recreation for Southwest Kansans. The idea of some admitted "odd ducks" about fifteen years ago, the sport has captured the fancy of young and old alike.

Equipment is minimal. A new or used tank that doesn't leak, will do. Fancier models have milk crates or lawn chairs added for comfort. A

Amaranth Banana Bread

½ cup Cheyenne Gap® Amaranth Flour
1½ cups whole wheat flour
1 tsp baking powder
½ tsp baking soda
2 eggs, beaten
½ cup melted butter
½ cup Schmidt Honey
1 tsp vanilla extract
1 cup mashed bananas
1 cup chopped walnuts

- Combine dry ingredients in a large bowl.
- Beat eggs, butter, honey, vanilla and bananas together; add all at once to flour mixture.
- Mix just until dry ingredients are moistened.
- Stir in walnuts.
- Pour batter into a buttered and floured 9" x 5" loaf pan.
- Bake in 350 degree oven for 60-65 minutes.
- Cover with foil if loaf is browning too fast.
- Makes 1 loaf.

Quick Country Herb Bread

2 cups The Wheat Bin Kwik Mix
1 tbsp Rabbit Creek Country Herb Dip Mix
2 tbsp sugar
⅔ cup milk
1 egg

- Preheat oven to 375 degrees.
- Combine all ingredients until soft dough forms; beat vigorously 30 seconds.
- Place dough in a well greased 8" x 4" loaf pan.
- Bake 30 minutes.
- Serve warm.
- Makes 1 loaf.

cooler, amply provisioned with beverages, also adds to the enjoyment.

Once launched, a fully-crewed tank has a draft of six to eight inches. Surprisingly stable, the craft relies on the river current for power.

Runs from the most popular launching site afford a trip of about two hours before reaching the bridge south of Syracuse. Add paddlers and time is shortened. Add a motor, as one fellow did, and spend a lot time going in circles. Tanks without rudders are hard to steer.

Tankin', like other sports, has its own lingo. The two key words for the novice are "duck" and "mallard." When someone hollers either it's best to crouch down to avoid the thorny Russian olive branches that line the riverbank.

Water fights are another certainty. Few tankers can resist cooling off other crews they encounter. Newcomers to the sport are guaranteed a baptism.

The Chamber of Commerce sponsors Syracuse River Run annually during the last weekend in July. Everyone is welcome to enter.

NORTHWEST KANSAS

Northwest Kansas was covered by Cretaceous seas one hundred million years ago. Large marine animals swam in the depths while huge reptiles flew overhead. Changing conditions brought other exotic animals to the region. As recently as a few thousand years ago, elephants, camels and rhinoceros lived there. An abundance of their fossils, in the exposed rocks of the area, has made Northwest Kansas a favorite destination for paleontologists and has led to the establishment of several unique museum collections.

Indians were the first human inhabitants of the region. They were replaced by buffalo hunters, soldiers, railroad workers, desperados and ordinary citizens. Soon towns sprang up to supply the commodities and goods that couldn't be grown or made on the hundreds of family farms nearby. Increased prosperity came with an oil boom in the 1930's.

Today, Northwest Kansas' economy continues to be sustained,

Cracked Wheat Honey Bread

2 pkgs active dry yeast
2¼ cups warm water, divided
½ cup Sperry Apiaries Honey
¼ cup shortening
2 tsp salt
½ cup The Wheat Bin Cracked Wheat
4 cups The Wheat Bin Stone Ground Whole Wheat Flour
2-3 cups HearTland Mill® Unbleached White Flour

- Dissolve yeast in ½ cup warm water in large mixing bowl.
- Add rest of ingredients except the unbleached flour, including remaining warm water.
- Mix well, 2-3 minutes.
- Let stand 12 minutes.
- Mix in enough unbleached flour to make dough easy to handle.
- Turn onto lightly floured board; knead until smooth, about 10 minutes.
- Place in lightly greased bowl; turn greased side up.
- Cover and let rise until doubled in size, about 1 hour.
- Punch down and divide into halves.
- Form loaves; let rise until doubled.
- Place into 2 greased 8″ x 4″ loaf pans.
- Bake in 375 degree oven for 40-45 minutes.
- Cool on wire racks.
- Makes 2 loaves.

Whole Wheat Brown Bread

2 cups W-R Whole Wheat Flour
2 tbsp Kretschmer Wheat Germ
½ cup W-R Unbleached Flour
1 tsp baking powder
1 tsp baking soda
1 tsp Carey Salt
1½ cups Steffen's Buttermilk
¼ cup Rainbow Honey Farm Honey
¼ cup molasses

- Combine all ingredients. Stir just until batter is well moistened, about 70 strokes.
- Pour into greased 9″ x 5″ loaf pan.
- Bake in 350 degree oven for 50-60 minutes, until toothpick inserted into center comes out clean.
- Remove immediately from pan to wire rack for cooling.
- Makes 1 loaf.

Whole Wheat Pumpkin Quick Bread

1½ cups sugar

½ cup melted butter

2 Sunnyfresh Farms Eggs

1 cup canned pumpkin

½ cup water

1¼ cups all-purpose flour

¾ cup Old Dutch Mill Whole Wheat Flour

1 tsp baking soda

¼ tsp baking powder

½ tsp salt

½ tsp ginger

½ tsp cinnamon

½ tsp cloves

½ tsp nutmeg

½ cup chopped Kansas Nutworks Pecans

- Mix sugar and butter together until well blended.
- Add eggs, pumpkin and water; mix thoroughly.
- Sift dry ingredients together; add to pumpkin mixture and stir until moistened.
- Stir in walnuts.
- Pour into greased 9″ x 5″ loaf pan and bake in 350 degree oven for 70 minutes, or until done.
- Remove from pan and cool on wire rack.
- Cool thoroughly before slicing.
- Makes 1 loaf.

Quick Dilly Bread

½ cup butter

1 tbsp Rabbit Creek Dill Dip Mix

1 loaf frozen white bread dough, thawed

- Grease well an 8″ x 4″ loaf pan.
- Melt butter and stir in dip mix.
- Divide the loaf into 12 equal pieces; shape each into a ball.
- Roll each ball in the butter mixture.
- Put 8 balls in a single layer in bottom of the prepared pan.
- Arrange the remaining 4 balls down the center.
- Cover; let rise in warm spot about 1 hour or until doubled in size.
- Bake in 375 degree oven for 30-35 minutes, until golden brown.
- Makes 12 servings.

to a large degree, by agriculture and oil. Tourism also is making its mark.

Northwest Kansas has many tourist attractions that would be world famous if they were located near major population centers such as New York City, Chicago or Los Angeles. The Garden of Eden, for example, has earned international notoriety. Art connoisseurs have described the Garden as "one of America's finest examples of primitive art."

I've visited the Lucas, Kansas, attraction many times and like the thousands of people who see it each year, I still go away shaking my head in disbelief. Crude. Bizarre. Fascinating. It's all of these. And more.

The Garden of Eden is the creation of Samuel Perry Dinsmoor, a disabled Civil War veteran. Biblical themes and the events of the 1800's and early 1900's are depicted in a most unusual fashion. Huge concrete trees . . . some thirty to forty feet tall . . . are adorned with animals, angels, devils and human characters he fashioned to interpret his themes.

Dinsmoor's political commentaries are of life as he saw it. In one, the Goddess of Liberty is designed to reflect his belief that trust companies were getting too big and powerful and would bring down civilization. The Goddess is shown driving a spear through the head of the trusts. Below her the people, through their votes, are portrayed sawing down the "chartered rights limb" on which the trusts stand.

Another tree depicts labor being crucified by a lawyer, a doctor, a preacher and a banker.

"I do not say they are all grafters," Dinsmoor wrote in his book, *Pictorial History of the Cabin Home,* "but I do say they are the leaders of all who eat cake by the sweat of the other fellow's face. The lawyer interprets the law. The Doctor has his knife and saw ready to carve up the bones. The Preacher is saying to this poor fellow crucified, 'Never mind your suffering here on earth, my friend, secure home in heaven for A-l-l E-t-e-r-n-i-t-y and you'll be all right.' This is the stuff he is giving Labor

No-Knead Refrigerator Rolls

1 cup hot water

½ cup shortening

¼ cup sugar

1 tsp salt

1 pkg active dry yeast

½ cup warm water, 90 degrees

1 egg

3 cups Old Dutch Mill Flour

- Place hot water in large bowl and stir in shortening, sugar and salt.
- Cool; dissolve yeast in warm water and let stand 3-5 minutes.
- Beat in egg.
- Add these ingredients to shortening mixture.
- Add flour, beating the dough for 2 minutes (dough will be soft until chilled).
- Refrigerate in a greased container and cover.
- This dough will keep in refrigerator for approximately 5 days.
- Shape rolls with greased hands approximately 1 hour before baking.
- Allow rolls to double in size.
- Bake rolls in a preheated 425 degree oven for about 15 minutes.
- Makes 18 rolls.

Sunshine Cinnamon Rolls

2 pkgs Best of the Sweet Country Popcorn Bread Mix

¼ cup melted butter

1 tbsp cinnamon

1 cup brown sugar

¼ cup raisins (optional)

¼ cup chopped Carden Pecans (optional)

powdered sugar icing

- Prepare mix according to pkg directions. Cover dough; let rise until doubled.
- Knead down and roll bread out to 15″ x 9″ rectangle.
- Spread with melted butter and sprinkle with mixture of cinnamon, sugar, raisins and nuts, if desired.
- Roll up tightly from 15″ side. Pinch dough to seal edges; cut into 1″-1½″ portions.
- Put in greased cake pan until double in size. (To help this, put a pan of hot water on the bottom rack of the oven.)
- When doubled, bake in 350 degree oven for 25 minutes.
- Ice with powdered sugar icing.
- Makes 1 doz rolls.

for his cake. He knows nothing about Eternity, and that he does know, if he knows anything. What fools we be to sweat to give the other fellow cake. The banker has the money, takes the interest and breaks up more people than any other class."

To understand Dinsmoor's mammoth work one needs to know more about the eccentric native of Ohio who moved to the Great Plains.

Above all, Samuel Perry Dinsmoor was a showman. In 1870 at the age of 27, he married his first wife, a wealthy widow. The ceremony was performed while both the bride and groom were on horseback. She bore him four children and it wasn't until they all reached maturity that Samuel was permitted access to his wife's money. To fund his Garden of Eden project he used the two military pensions he received — one to which he was entitled, the other a result of a bookkeeping error.

"Mr. Dinsmoor wasn't dishonest," said Jacob Wolpert, a long-time tour guide at the Garden of Eden who knew the man personally. "When he started getting the second military pension check he immediately notified the government of the mistake. Well, you know how bureaucrats are today in this age of computers. They were no different then when everything was done manually. They informed Mr. Dinsmoor that it was impossible for them to make an error and he continued to get two checks for the rest of his life."

When Dinsmoor decided to build his home in Lucas, showman that he was, he wanted it to stand out from all others. His idea was to construct a log cabin out of stone instead of wood. He quarried limestone planks by hand and transported them to town by horse-drawn wagon. Each log was then notched and fitted together to create a unique structure. All but five of the stones ran the full length of the home. The largest measuring twenty-one feet!

Inside, the former teacher and farmer designed the main floor to be a tourist attraction. Featured in this show area are windows and doors of varied sizes, some side by side. Ornate pressed wood molding was used for door and window frames and baseboard. Much of the furniture was of Dinsmoor's own manufacture. The home's second story and basement

Whole Wheat Cinnamon Rolls

2 pkgs active dry yeast
1 tsp sugar
2 cups warm water, 90 degrees, divided
¾ cup vegetable oil
⅔ cup Sunflower State Brand Honey
1½ tsp salt
2 eggs
6 cups Heartland Mill® Whole Wheat Flour
melted butter, sugar, cinnamon, brown sugar, pecans, raisins

- Dissolve yeast and sugar in 1 cup warm water.
- Add oil, honey, salt, eggs, remaining 1 cup water and 2 cups flour.
- Beat 5 minutes at medium speed.
- Add remaining flour; beat 5 minutes at slow speed.
- Let rise until doubled.
- Roll out and cover lightly with butter, sugar, cinnamon, and brown sugar; sprinkle with pecans or raisins.
- Roll up and cut into 1″ thick rolls.
- Place into buttered baking pan, and bake in 375 degree oven until golden brown.
- Makes 2 doz rolls.

No-Knead Whole Wheat Rolls

1 pkg active dry yeast
¼ cup warm water, 90 degrees
1 cup Steffen's Milk, scalded
½ cup butter or margarine
¼ cup sugar
1 tsp salt
1¾ cups The Wheat Bin Stone Ground Whole Wheat Flour
1 egg, well beaten
1¾ cups unbleached flour

- Dissolve yeast in water.
- Pour hot milk over butter or margarine, sugar and salt. Let cool.
- Add whole wheat flour; beat well for 3 minutes with mixer.
- Add yeast and egg; beat with mixer until smooth.
- Add unbleached flour. (Add more flour if dough is too soft.)
- Let rise until doubled.
- Stir down and let rise again.
- Stir down and shape into dinner rolls or sweet rolls.
- Place rolls on cookie sheet and bake in 375 degree oven for 12-15 minutes, or until lightly browned.
- Makes 2 doz rolls.

were used for living quarters.

The home, the first stage of his project, was completed in 1910. Then, nearing 70 years of age, he began his seventeen-year labor on the Garden.

Dinsmoor's first wife died in 1917. In the spring of 1924, at the age of 81, he married his 20-year-old housekeeper. That union later resulted in a son and a daughter.

Even in death the eccentric creator of the Garden of Eden wanted to put on a good show. His self-made concrete coffin has a glass lid through which more adventuresome tourists can view him in repose.

"I have a will that none except my widow, my descendants, their husbands and wives, shall go in to see me for less than one dollar. That will pay someone to look after the place."

All money is exchanged outside of the mausoleum.

As for the concrete coffin, and the two gallon jug at its foot, Dinsmoor offered the following explanations.

"It seems to me that people buried in iron and wooden boxes will be frying and burning up in the resurrection morn. How will they get out when this world is on fire? Cement will not stand fire, the glass will break. The lid will fly open and I will sail out like a locust. Some people know they are going to heaven and those they do not like are going to hell. I am going where the Boss puts me."

And where is that? Enter the cement jug.

"In the resurrection morn, if I have to go below, I'll go below, I'll grab my jug and fill it with water on the road down."

After visiting the Garden of Eden I recommend that you make another stop in Lucas at Brandt's Market. Local residents know the Brandts make fine sausages from scratch, and they have spread the word. Now people passing through stop to make purchases. Before buying, try a free sample or two of the secret recipe meats.

Southern Style Hush Puppies

1 cup Old Dutch Mill Corn Meal
½ tsp salt
1 tsp baking powder
¾ cup milk
1 Sunnyfresh Farms Egg, lightly beaten
¼ cup chopped onion
vegetable oil to fry

- Mix together dry ingredients; add milk, egg and chopped onion.
- Heat oil in deep skillet.
- Form small balls; drop into hot oil.
- Fry for 5-6 minutes or until golden brown and crisp.
- Drain on paper towels.
- Serves 4-6.

Apple Kuchen

2 cups HearTland Mill® Buttermilk Pancake & Waffle Mix
½ cup brown sugar
½ cup butter
1 egg
½ tsp vanilla extract
4-5 Champlin's Orchard Cooking Apples

- Pour mix into medium bowl; stir in brown sugar.
- Cut in butter with a pastry cutter until mixture resembles coarse corn meal.
- Beat the egg with vanilla and add to first mixture.
- Work together with your hands or wooden spoon.
- Divide dough in half. Press half into bottom and up sides of a pie pan.
- Slice and core apples and cover the crust completely.
- With the remaining dough, roll into ½" balls and place on top of apples.
- Bake in 350 degree oven for 30 minutes.
- Cool before slicing.
- Serves 8.

Hays is the largest population center in Northwest Kansas. If you watched "Gunsmoke" on television, as I did, you may recall Marshall Matt Dillon headed to Hays City. Usually he had a prisoner in tow, bound for frontier justice.

Hays City was built near Fort Hays, an unusual military post of its time because, unlike typical forts of the earlier eastern frontier, it had no stockade or fortification wall. Only a stone blockhouse afforded protection. No matter though, the post was never attacked.

Four original structures remain at the Kansas State Historical Society attraction. Two are officers' quarters. There's also a guardhouse and the unique blockhouse, hexagonal in shape, with two wings extending north and south.

Constructed in 1865, the military post was named in honor of General Alexander Hays who had been killed a year earlier in the Civil War Battle of the Wilderness. Garrison strength normally averaged three companies, about two hundred ten men, both cavalry and infantry.

As the threat of Indian attack diminished, Fort Hays became a quartermaster depot supplying other forts throughout the West and Southwest. Civilian personnel complemented the military and nearby Hays City grew into a wild town. For a time, according to Elizabeth Custer whose husband was serving at the fort, "there was enough desperate history in that little town to make a whole library of dime novels."

Fort Hays was abandoned in 1889 and in 1897 it was given to the State of Kansas. Living history demonstrations are presented there on some Sunday afternoons.

Do you believe in ghosts? Fort Hays supposedly has one.

Like most of us, John Schmidt probably never expected to see a ghost. An ordinary man, the long-time Hays resident labored on his family farm

Kansas Toast

3 eggs, beaten
2 tbsp milk
2 tbsp orange-pineapple juice concentrate
⅛ tsp cinnamon
2 tsp sugar
8 thick slices "SunnyWheat" Bread
2 tbsp butter, divided
syrup or fruit preserves

- Beat all ingredients except bread and butter until well blended.
- Melt 1 tbsp butter in skillet over medium heat.
- Dip bread in egg mixture coating both sides.
- Cook in skillet for 2-3 minutes on both sides.
- Serve with syrup or fruit preserves.
- Serves 4.

Bread Sticks

1 (1.75 lb) pkg "SunnyWheat" Bread Mix
3 pkgs active dry yeast
1½ cups warm water, 90 degrees
1 cup melted butter
½ tsp garlic salt

- Make bread according to pkg directions until shaping.
- Divide dough into 4 equal portions; cover all but 1 portion to prevent the dough from drying out.
- Divide portion into 8 parts. Roll each part to 3″ in length.
- Place on a lightly greased cookie sheet about ½″ apart.
- Mix butter and garlic salt together; brush on each stick.
- Continue until all dough is shaped. Cover and place in warm area until doubled.
- Brush again with garlic butter and bake in 375 degree oven for 8-10 minutes or until brown.
- If desired, brush hot bread sticks with garlic butter again before serving.
- Makes 32 bread sticks.

and worked a second job at nearby Fort Hays State College.

One morning, just after dawn, the farmer glanced up from his chores and saw a tall woman walking across the grasslands from the abandoned old fort. Her gait was stately. What seemed odd, to him, was her clothing. She wore an ankle length blue dress and a sun bonnet, outdated attire for western Kansas in the current year of 1917.

Schmidt couldn't make out the woman's face as she headed for a line shack about one-quarter of a mile from a site locals called the "lonely grave." His shouts to her went unheeded. She kept walking.

Schmidt mounted his horse to go after the woman. Oddly enough, the animal reared up and tried to bolt from him. His dog began yelping and scampered for home. The horse followed.

Schmidt's family saw everything that happened, including the woman entering the line shack. Throughout the day they took turns watching for her to emerge but she never did.

Finally the Schmidts decided to march as a family to the line shack and confront the stranger. Upon their arrival they found the door secured by a rusty lock . . . on the outside.

John kicked in the door and the Schmidts looked around. Not even the dust had been disturbed. The woman was not there!

Schmidt later related his story to the fort's caretaker, George Brown, who theorized that the woman could have been Elizabeth Polly, a former resident of the fort. The improbability of that assumption was that Mrs. Polly had been dead for fifty years.

Elizabeth Polly and her husband Ephriam, were newlyweds in 1867, when he brought her from Liberty, Missouri, to the remote western outpost of Fort Hays. With social life being limited for a lowly paid military hospital steward, the young couple spent many evenings walking out to a nearby hilltop where they could watch activity at the busy fort and watch passersby on the well-traversed trails of the surrounding countryside.

Cracked Wheat Muffins

1 cup The Granary Cracked Wheat
1 cup hot milk
1 egg
¼ cup vegetable oil
1¼ cups all-purpose flour
1 tbsp baking powder
¼ tsp salt
½ cup sugar

- Combine cracked wheat and milk; cover and let soak 5 minutes to overnight.
- Preheat oven to 375 degrees.
- Grease or line 12 medium muffin cups.
- Beat egg and oil into cracked wheat mixture.
- Sift together dry ingredients in mixing bowl. Add egg mixture until just moistened.
- Spoon into cups, filling ⅔ full.
- Bake in 375 degree oven for 20-25 minutes, until golden brown.
- Makes 12 muffins.

Blueberry Muffins

2 cups W-R All-Purpose Flour
1½ cups sugar
¾ cup shortening
2 tsp baking powder
1 cup milk
1 tsp salt
1 tsp vanilla extract
1½ cups fresh Buckets of Berries Blueberries

- Preheat oven to 375 degrees.
- Blend together flour, sugar and shortening. Take out 1 cup and reserve.
- Mix in baking powder, milk, salt and vanilla, and fill muffin pans half full.
- Top each muffin with blueberries, and spoon on part of reserved mixture.
- Bake in 375 degree oven for 18 minutes.
- Makes 12 muffins.

When an epidemic of cholera broke out at Fort Hays, Elizabeth joined her husband in helping to care for the sick. She, too, became afflicted with the disease that was nearly always fatal in those times. After lingering for days she died.

While on her deathbed Elizabeth repeatedly pleaded to her husband that he bury her atop the hill so special to them. Her wish was granted. She was laid to rest there dressed in her favorite blue dress and bonnet.

For years the grave remained unmarked except for a wooden cross erected by a Boy Scout troop in the early 1900's. Locals claim that on some evenings, even today, an eerie blue light hangs over the spot. Is it Elizabeth's soul? Is she waiting there for her lost mate? Or, does she still walk near Fort Hays in search of Ephriam as George Brown surmised?

The first frontier cemetery to be known as Boot Hill was located in Hays City. Occasionally someone would be interred there, having died of natural causes. More than likely their demise was due to gunfights, knifings, suicide or alcoholism.

Hays City had saloons aplenty. They included Kate Coffey's, Waters and Murray's, Ed Goddard's and Tommy Drum's, not to mention other establishments like Cy Goddard's Dance Hall, notorious even by Hays City standards. It is said that James Butler "Wild Bill" Hickok mortally wounded a fellow there in 1869.

William Cody also lived in Hays City during the late 1860's. As construction continued on the Union Pacific Railroad headed west he was hired to kill twelve buffalo a day for food. The job earned him the nickname "Buffalo Bill."

In the 1870's Volga Germans began arriving in the Hays City area. These German-speaking Catholics left Russia to avoid conscription in

Multi-Grain Muffins
"Celebrate! Kansas Food" Contest Winner

1 cup rolled oats
1 cup Steffen's Buttermilk
1 Sunnyfresh Farms Egg
½ cup brown sugar
⅓ cup vegetable oil
¼ cup W-R Whole Wheat Flour
¼ cup W-R Unbleached Flour
¼ cup bran
¼ cup Kretschmer Wheat Germ
⅛ cup sesame seeds
1 tsp Carey Salt
1 tsp baking powder
½ tsp baking soda

- Combine oats, buttermilk, egg, sugar and oil; set aside.
- Combine other ingredients; blend thoroughly.
- Stir dry ingredients into oat mixture.
- Fill paper-lined muffin tins ⅔ full. Bake in 400 degree oven for 15-20 minutes, until lightly browned.
- Makes 12 muffins.

Southwestern Style Muffins
"Celebrate! Kansas Food" Contest Winner

2 cups The Wheat Bin Kwik Mix
¼ cup vegetable oil
1 egg
1 tsp Williams Chili Seasoning
¼ tsp Carey Salt
1 cup The Whole Enchilada's Salsa, drained
¼ cup milk
1½ cups grated Alma Cheddar Cheese

- Line 12 cup muffin pan with paper baking cups.
- Combine all ingredients except cheese, until moistened. (Batter will be lumpy.)
- Fold in cheese.
- Fill muffin cups ⅔ full.
- Bake in 400 degree oven about 20 minutes, until golden brown.
- Makes 12 muffins.

the armies of Catherine the Great. A peace-loving lot, they took up farming. Among their legacies are some magnificent native stone churches in nearby communities such as Schoenchen, Liebenthal and Victoria.

The Romanesque-style St. Fidelis church in Victoria earned the title "Cathedral of the Plains." Completed in 1911, it is constructed of limestone—the same material used in the many stone fence posts, or "post rocks," you see lining the highways of the region.

Hays, as the city is now referred, is a major retail center for much of western Kansas. It is also home to Fort Hays State University, a former National Association of Intercollegiate Athletics men's basketball champion.

The Sternberg Museum on the Fort Hays State campus is noted for its Hall of Paleontology which contains several outstanding specimens of prehistoric Kansas inhabitants. Among them is the most complete and best preserved Trinacromerum skeleton ever discovered.

The Trinacromerum, a short-necked Plesiosaur, had a small head, oval body, and legs that resembled paddles. It swam on the surface of the Cretaceous Sea in Northwest Kansas, or just below it, feeding on fish and squid-like belemnoids.

The museum's highlight, however, is the fossilized "fish within a fish."

One day, long before recorded time, a fourteen-foot Portheus was searching for food in the Kansas waters. The snub-faced fish, sometimes called the "bulldog tarpon," encountered a six-foot Gillecus and swallowed it whole. What must have seemed like a gourmet meal to Portheus turned out to be fatal. Researchers think it probably died while attempting to digest the large fish.

Portheus and Gillecus, now one for eternity, sank to the bottom of the sea. They remained there until 1925 when George Sternberg, collecting

Ever-Ready Bran Muffins

1 (15 oz) pkg bran flakes with raisins
5 cups W-R All-Purpose Flour
3 cups sugar
1 tbsp plus 2 tsp baking soda
2 tsp salt
4 eggs, beaten
1 qt Steffen's Buttermilk
1 cup vegetable oil

- Combine bran flakes, flour, sugar, baking soda and salt in a very large bowl; make a well in center of mixture.
- Add eggs, buttermilk and oil; stir enough to moisten dry ingredients.
- Cover and store in refrigerator until ready to bake. (Batter can be kept in refrigerator up to 6 weeks).
- To bake, spoon batter into greased muffin pans, filling ⅔ full.
- Bake in 400 degree oven for 12-15 minutes.
- Makes 5 doz muffins.

Amaranth Pancakes

¼ cup Cheyenne Gap® Amaranth Flour
1¼ cups all-purpose flour
¾ tsp salt
3 tbsp sugar
3½ tsp baking powder
1¼ cups Steffen's Milk
1 egg, well beaten
3 tbsp vegetable oil

- Sift dry ingredients together.
- Mix together milk, egg and oil, and combine with the flour mixture. Stir, do not beat.
- Makes 1 doz pancakes.

Amaranth Biscuits

⅓ cup Cheyenne Gap® Amaranth Flour
1⅔ cups W-R All-Purpose Flour
4 tsp baking powder
½ tsp salt
½ tsp cream of tartar
2 tbsp sugar
½ cup shortening
⅔ cup milk

- Mix together dry ingredients.
- Cut in shortening until it resembles a coarse mixture.
- Stir in milk.
- Form into ball and knead 10-12 times.
- Pat or roll out on a floured surface until ¾" thick. Cut with cutter.
- Bake in 450 degree oven for 10-12 minutes.
- Makes 1 doz biscuits.

in a Gove County cretaceous chalk bed, unearthed their remarkably complete remains.

Both the Portheus and the Gillecus must have lived in fear of the Mosasaur, a large sea-going lizard that also roamed Kansas waters. A veritable eating machine, the reptile had snake-like skin, flippers instead of legs, and propelled itself by thrashing its tail. The species sometimes reached lengths of sixty feet. The Sternberg's Mosasaur is just over thirty feet long.

The museum's Hall of Natural History contains specimens of various modern animals. Highlights are two dioramas, one depicting a lion walking across the East African Plains. It serves as a contrast to the present plains of western Kansas and as a model for what the Hays region may have looked like a few million years ago. The second diorama depicts western Kansas in the 1850's.

L ebanon, Kansas, sits smack dab in the middle of the forty-eight contiguous states. It was the center of the nation until Alaska and Hawaii entered the picture.

Lebanon is small (population 440) so if you're having trouble locating it on your map just trace Highway 183 north from Hays to Phillipsburg. Take a right on Highway 36, go through Smith Center and, just to the east, voila! You're 1,630 miles from Boston and 1,630 miles from San Francisco.

The geodetic center of North America also is in Northwest Kansas. Don't put your maps away yet! Look straight south from Lebanon to the town of Osborne. One mile to the north of Osborne is a park with a Kansas Historical Marker that states:

> On a ranch 18 miles southeast of this marker a bronze plate marks the most important spot on this continent to surveyors and map makers. Engraved in the bronze is a cross-mark and on the tiny point where the

Banana Split Pancakes

1 (1 lb) pkg Best of the Sweet Country Popcorn Pancake Mix, Wheat Pancake Mix or Oat Bran Pancake Mix

1½ cups Elm Creek Honey

2 bananas

1 cup fresh Sargeant Strawberry Farm Strawberries

1 (8 oz) ctn whipped topping

¼ cup peanuts

strawberries to garnish

- Prepare mix according to pkg directions.
- Heat honey in microwave or oven until hot.
- Slice bananas in the honey and spoon over pancakes.
- Top with strawberries and whipped topping.
- Sprinkle with peanuts.
- Garnish with strawberries.
- Serves 4-6.

Crazy Quilt Bread

3 eggs, beaten

½ cup vegetable oil

½ cup milk

2½ cups HearTland Mill® Unbleached White Flour

1 cup sugar

1 tsp baking powder

1 tsp baking soda

1 tsp cinnamon

½ tsp Carey Salt

2 cups shredded Emerald Garden Carrots

¾ cup shredded coconut

½ cup chopped maraschino cherries

½ cup raisins

½ cup chopped Carden Pecans

½ cup Kretschmer Wheat Germ

- Blend eggs, oil and milk.
- In large bowl, sift together flour, sugar, baking powder, baking soda, cinnamon and salt.
- Add egg mixture; mix just until thoroughly combined.
- Stir in remaining ingredients.
- Pour into 4 well greased and floured (16 oz) fruit or vegetable cans.
- Bake in 350 degree oven 45-50 minutes. For 1 large loaf, bake in 9" x 5" loaf pan for 55-60 minutes.
- Remove bread and cool thoroughly.
- Makes 4 small loaves or 1 large loaf.

"Kansas, in sum, is one of our finest
states and lives a sane, peaceful
and prosperous life."

Pearl S. Buck
America

Amelia Earhart's homestead, Atchison

Apple Tea Bread

½ cup butter
¾ cup sugar
3 eggs
2 cups W-R All-Purpose Flour
1 tsp baking powder
½ tsp salt
½ tsp cinnamon
¼ tsp nutmeg
1 cup applesauce
6 tbsp Golden Mill Sorghum
1 cup raisins
½ cup chopped nuts
1 (3 oz) pkg cream cheese, softened
2 tbsp sugar

- In a large bowl, cream butter and ¾ cup sugar until light and fluffy.
- Add eggs, one at a time, beating well after each addition.
- Combine dry ingredients; set aside.
- Combine applesauce and sorghum.
- Add dry ingredients alternately with applesauce mixture to egg mixture; fold in raisins and nuts.
- Turn into 4 individual size loaf pans that have been well greased. If desired, this can be baked in 9¼" x 5¼" x 2¾" bread pan.
- Bake small loaves 30 minutes in 350 degree oven, the large loaf for 1 hour, or until a toothpick inserted in center comes out clean.
- Cool 10 minutes; remove from pans and cool on wire racks.
- Combine cream cheese and 2 tbsp sugar.
- Serve with sweetened cream cheese spread.
- Makes 4 individual loaves or 1 full-size loaf.

Beer Bread

3 cups W-R Self-Rising Flour
3 tsp sugar
1 can warm beer
melted butter

- Stir all ingredients together until just mixed, being careful not to over stir.
- Put in an ungreased 8" x 4" loaf pan in cold oven.
- Turn oven to 350 degrees and bake for 70 minutes.
- Take out of bread pan and drizzle with melted butter.
- Makes 1 loaf.

lines cross depend the surveys of a sixth of the world's surface. This is the Geodetic Center of the United States, the 'Primary Station' for all North American surveys. It was located in 1901 by the U.S. Coast and Geodetic Survey. Later, Canada and Mexico adopted the point and its supporting system as the base for their surveys and it is now known as the 'North American Datum.' What Greenwich is to the Longitude of the world, therefore, a Kansas pasture is to the lines and boundaries of this continent. . .

Afever ran rampant throughout the South in the 1870's and 1880's. Afflicting only Blacks, it spread from cities to rural hamlets, to the countryside, leaving few people unscathed. Those who did not succumb to the malady were supportive of those who did. By word of mouth, posters and pamphlets, they informed each other of the only place where a cure could be found. Kansas, a prairie land few of them had ever seen, offered their only hope.

"Kansas Fever" reached its pitch in the years 1878-1882, when more than twenty thousand Blacks landed on the levees at Kansas City, determined to make a new life for themselves and their descendants. Although Black migration to the state had been going on for years, this huge influx was the most remarkable migration in the United States after the Civil War.

Those Blacks who migrated to Kansas when the fever was at its pitch were labeled "Exodusters." This coined term took note that theirs was a migratory movement and that their skills were primarily tied to the land, being agricultural in nature. The label is proudly used by their descendants, to this day, in referring to these ancestors.

Nicodemus was the longest lasting of the all-Black communities of the Exoduster movement. It was established in 1877 and, while a ghost

Whole Wheat Granola Coffeecake
"Celebrate! Kansas Food" Contest Winner

½ cup W-R Unbleached Flour

1¼ cups W-R Whole Wheat Flour

1 tsp baking soda

½ tsp Carey Salt

1 Sunnyfresh Farms Egg

1 cup Steffen's Buttermilk

¼ cup melted Steffen's Butter

½ cup Friesen Honey Farms Honey

Topping:

¼ cup W-R Whole Wheat Flour

¼ cup brown sugar

¾ cup Sun Country Granola

½ cup chopped pecans

1 tsp cinnamon

¼ cup melted Steffen's Butter

- Preheat oven to 375 degrees.
- Mix flours, baking soda and salt.
- In a separate, large bowl, beat egg until very light; add the buttermilk, butter and honey. Beat well to blend.
- Add flour mixture and fold gently until just combined.
- Spread batter smoothly in a buttered 8″ square pan.
- To make topping, combine first 5 ingredients. Drizzle with melted butter and toss.
- Sprinkle with topping and bake 25-30 minutes, or until toothpick inserted in middle comes out clean.
- Serve warm.
- Makes 16 servings.

Golden Dinner Bread

⅔ cup Steffen's Milk

½ cup Steffen's butter

¼ cup water

4 cups Old Dutch Mill All-Purpose Flour, divided

1 cup pumpkin

⅓ cup granulated sugar

1 pkg active dry yeast

1 tsp salt

3 eggs, lightly beaten

- Combine milk, butter and water.
- Heat to melt butter; cool.
- Combine milk mixture, 1½ cups flour, pumpkin, sugar, yeast, and salt.
- Beat on high speed 2 minutes.
- Stir in remaining flour.
- Cover and let rise in warm, draft-free place for 30 to 40 minutes, or until doubled in bulk.
- Spoon into greased, 10″ tube pan.
- Cover and let rise in warm, draft-free place 30 to 40 minutes.
- Bake in 350 degree oven 30 to 40 minutes, or until golden brown.
- Remove from pan; cool.
- Serves 10-12.

of its former self, exists today near Hill City. Although the colonists lacked sufficient tools, seed and money, they managed to survive the first winter by selling buffalo bones and working for the Kansas Pacific Railroad.

Their industriousness brought approving notices in Kansas newspapers. One story concerned a farmer who with a single cow "broke" and improved twelve acres of prairie and cultivated eight acres of corn. Another spaded a four-foot hedge row around one hundred sixty acres of land.

As the settlement became more permanent, the pioneers erected "soddies," the traditional homes of most early prairie settlers. These were dugouts excavated three or four feet into the earth and finished above with blocks of sod taken from the surrounding land.

One of the most interesting things about Nicodemus is how the settlement got its name. It was not, as many believed, derived from the Biblical Nicodemus. Rather, it was a tribute to a legendary slave and prophet who reportedly arrived on the second slave ship to reach America and later purchased his freedom. A song, celebrating him, was sung by plantation slaves:

> Nicodemus was a slave of African birth,
>> And was bought for a bag full of gold;
> He was reckoned a part of the salt of the earth,
>> But he died years ago, very old.
> Nicodemus was a prophet, at least he was as wise,
>> For he told of the battles to come;
> How we trembled with fear, when he rolled up his eyes,
>> And we heeded the shake of his thumb.

The most prominent of all Black politicians to emerge from Nicodemus was E.P. McCabe. He became state auditor in 1882 and was re-elected in 1884.

By 1887, Nicodemus had churches, stores, lodges, a school and two newspapers. Failure of a railroad to locate in the community sent it into a tailspin from which it never recovered.

SOUPS, STEWS & CHILI

Monument Rocks, Gove County

Photo by Loreen Locke McMillan

"Nicodemus might fade from the scene," one White newspaper man of the day wrote, "but to those who know the truth of history, the name will always recall the bravest attempt ever made by people of any color to establish homes in the high plains of Kansas."

Majestic pyramids rise abruptly from the Smoky Hill River Valley. The scene is not Egypt, however, it is Northwest Kansas.

Unique wind carved, water formations known as the Chalk Pyramids (or Monument Rocks depending on who you talk to), are made to order for those who want wide open spaces away from it all. The rock outcroppings rise to heights of sixty feet and are the sedimented remains of ancient marine life.

Located midway between Oakley and Scott City, the scenic area is nestled on a dirt and gravel road approximately five miles east of U.S. Highway 83. It was named the first national natural landmark in Kansas.

Until a few years ago the "Sphinx" kept a lonely vigil over the surroundings. Wind and rain eroded the fragile formation and much of it toppled.

Generally when I visit the pyramids no one is there. At most, I'll see a car or two. It's more likely I'll share the formations with deer (I've seen fifteen at one time), a scampering rabbit, a wily coyote, and ever-present hawks.

For the photo enthusiast, the pyramids offer a myriad of year-round opportunities. A good vantage point is on top of the bluffs north of the landmark. It's a fairly easy climb and you can capture the entire panorama. You'll also be captivated by an abandoned stone school nearby, and a picturesque windmill alongside the road.

Earnest and Vi Fick lived near the pyramids and spent much of their time roaming the area for fossils. They discovered more than

Taco Soup

1 (7 oz) pkg Soup Lady Bean Soup Mix
1 cup crumbled La Siesta Tortilla Chips
1-2 lbs Alma Cheddar Cheese, shredded
shredded lettuce (optional)

- Prepare soup mix according to #3 directions (Spicey Bean Pot).
- Ladle the hot soup into a large soup bowl or mug.
- Sprinkle chips, cheese and lettuce on top of the soup.
- Serve immediately.
- Serves 6-8.

Fresh Asparagus Soup

1 lb Pendleton's Fresh Asparagus, chopped
½ cup chopped fresh onion
1 (13 oz) can chicken broth, divided
2 tbsp butter
2 tbsp all-purpose flour
1 tsp salt
pepper to taste
1 cup Steffen's Milk
½ cup sour cream
1 tsp fresh lemon juice
Merritt Horticultural Center Fresh Chives to garnish

- Cook asparagus in covered saucepan with onion and ½ cup chicken broth 8-10 minutes, or until asparagus is just tender.
- Press through food mill or blend in electric blender until smooth.
- Melt butter; blend in flour, salt and pepper.
- Stir in remaining chicken broth.
- Cook over medium heat, stirring constantly, until mixture reaches boiling point.
- Stir in asparagus puree and milk.
- Stir a little of the mixture into sour cream; then stir back into the soup mixture.
- Add lemon juice.
- Heat just to serving temperature, stirring frequently.
- Garnish with fresh chives.
- Makes 4 cups.

Pony Express Station, Hanover

Hungarian Fresh Mushroom Soup

4 cups coarsely chopped Toto Cure of Kansas Fresh Mushrooms

2 tbsp bacon drippings

1 tbsp finely chopped onion

2 tsp salt

1 tsp paprika

¼ cup all-purpose flour

½ tsp Sunflower Organic Farm Chervil Leaves

6 cups chicken stock

1 egg, slightly beaten

½ cup sour cream

- Sauté mushrooms in bacon drippings with onion, salt and paprika in a large saucepan.
- Blend in flour and chervil.
- Add stock and mix well.
- Stir and cook until soup has thickened slightly.
- Blend egg with sour cream and add to soup.
- Heat thoroughly, stirring constantly.
- Makes 10 cups.

Smoked Sausage & Potato Chowder

1 tbsp butter

¼ cup chopped green onions

1 tsp Carey Salt

⅛ tsp white pepper

¼ tsp paprika

3 tbsp all-purpose flour

2⅓ cups water

1 cube chicken bouillon

2 cups Steffen's Milk

2 OhSe Smoked Polish Sausages, sliced

1 (16 oz) can Mexicorn, drained

3 cups frozen diced hash brown potatoes

1 tsp parsley flakes

- Melt butter in saucepan.
- Add green onions; cook until tender, about 5 minutes.
- Add seasonings and flour to onions and stir until absorbed.
- Cook 10 minutes on medium low heat; stir often.
- Add water and bouillon cube; stir until dissolved and smooth.
- Add milk; cook over medium heat until slightly thickened.
- Add sausage, Mexicorn and hash browns.
- Heat thoroughly over medium heat.
- Sprinkle individual portions with parsley.
- Serves 4-6.

eleven thousand shark's teeth plus crinoids, oyster shells—even petrified octopi—left from the era of the Cretaceous Sea.

Mrs. Fick was an excellent amateur artist who assembled the fossils into unique designs including the seals of the United States and Kansas. She also did melted wax paintings, paper mache, machine stitchery and wood carvings.

The Fick Fossil Museum in Oakley, which houses the Kansas couple's collection, was proclaimed by the *San Francisco Chronicle* as one of the twenty five great museums in the United States. Its other fossils include a fifteen-foot Portheus Molossus collected by paleontologist George F. Sternberg.

Oil paintings by local artists show the history and development of the Oakley area. There's also a replica of the 1886 Union Pacific depot that burned in 1940. A wall of cattlemen's brands accents an antique horse-drawn wagon.

Other exhibits include a general store that displays fine antiques and a sod house that is typical of the first settlers homes. The artifacts found at the site of Fort Monument are also interesting. Fascinating photographs of the area, taken by residents over the past ninety years, are mounted in several four-foot tall metal and glass albums.

Antique lovers find Colby's Prairie Museum of Art and History a treasure chest of glassware, porcelains, textiles, furnishings and dolls. A decade ago, its Kuska Collection was appraised by the Smithsonian Institution at more than one million dollars.

Among the museum's prized pieces is a massive hard-paste porcelain scene depicting "The Good Life" of the French aristocracy. Early American glass on display includes quality pieces manufactured using the cut, pressed, blown and molded methods. Steigel and Sandwich glass in cranberry, cobalt and vaseline colors; Steuben; and Tiffany are also represented. Art glass includes Galle, Burmese, Peachblow, Rubina

Sausage Soup

1 (14.75 oz) can chicken broth
1 (15.25 oz) can Great Northern or
other
white beans, drained
¾ cup water
½ cup uncooked, Pasta Mills Rigatoni
1 cup sliced Krehbiel's Polish Sausage
1 bay leaf
1 tbsp onion flakes
1 tsp parsley flakes

- Combine all ingredients in a saucepan.
- Bring to a boil and simmer 10 minutes.
- Serves 4.

Harvest Beef Stew

1 (3.25 oz) pkg Olde Westport Beef
Sauce Mix
4 cups water
1 (6 oz) can tomato paste
2 tomatoes, peeled and chopped
2 lbs Nutri-Beef Stew Meat, trimmed
1 small onion, chopped
3 Bismarck Gardens Carrots,
cut in ¼" slices
3 stalks celery, chopped
2 zucchini squash, cut in ½" slices
¼ head cabbage, sliced
2 potatoes, diced
½ tsp black pepper
Carey Salt (optional)

- In saucepan, prepare sauce mix according to pkg directions using 4 cups water, tomato paste and tomatoes.
- Bring to boil, stirring constantly, until thickened.
- Lower heat and simmer.
- Brown meat in skillet.
- Add onion to skillet; sauté until crisp tender.
- Transfer meat and sauce to a soup pot; add remaining ingredients.
- Add water, as needed, if too thick.
- Bring to boil over medium heat.
- Lower heat and simmer 30 minutes, or until vegetables are crisp tender.
- Adjust seasonings with salt and more pepper, if desired.
- Serves 6-8.

Verde, Quilted Mother-of-Pearl, satin glass, tortoiseshell and Millefiori.

Two of the two thousand dolls in the Kuska Collection are each valued at more than $50,000. One is a fashion doll signed by the famous doll maker Rocharde. The other, by the French designer Jumeau, is titled "The Sorceress." A mechanical marvel, the doll waves its wand to make three smaller dolls magically pop into view.

A gallery dedicated to Meissen, Europe's first and most important hard-paste factory, is a museum highlight. In the 1700's King August of Saxony and Poland hired a chemist to turn iron into gold. But paste was the best he could do.

Among other museum exhibits are English Ridgeway china with scenes from Charles Dickens' "Pickwick Papers," a case of silver, and Roman lamps found in Egypt and dating back two thousand years.

The Thomas County Historical Society operates the museum. Among its historical interpretations is "The Prairie Life . . . Conquering the Great American Desert." A sod house, representing the "soddies" built by homesteaders in the 1880's, includes furniture and clothing from the historical society's collection.

The museum building itself is a spectacular work of art. The structure was designed to fit into the landscape. Buffalo grass covers the earth berm and the roof is supported by concrete columns, not walls.

You probably don't recognize the name Brewster Higley. On the other hand, I'm fairly certain you've sung a poem of his that was set to music.

Higley was a practicing physician from Ohio who moved to a log cabin in Smith County. He would often while away his idle hours writing verse.

One spring day, in 1873, Higley was hunting along the banks of the Solomon River. As he laid in wait for a deer, he was distracted by the beauty surrounding him. In awe of what he saw, Higley put his rifle aside, took out a pencil and some paper, and began scribbling these lines:

Kansas City Steak Soup

3 cups water

2 tbsp instant minced onion

1 (10 oz) pkg frozen mixed vegetables

1 (14.5 oz) can whole tomatoes

1 lb ground beef, browned and drained

1 (.875 oz) pkg Williams Brown Gravy Mix

½ tsp pepper

1 tsp Carey Salt

½ cup melted Steffen's Butter

½ cup all-purpose flour

- Place all ingredients except butter and flour in a slow cooker.
- Cover and cook on low 8-10 hours (high, 4-5 hours).
- Turn to high 30 minutes before serving.
- Combine butter and flour; stir until smooth.
- Pour into slow cooker and blend well.
- Cook soup on high until thickened.
- Serves 4.

Slow Cooker Chili

4-4½ lbs Nutri-Beef Round Steak, trimmed and cut into ½" cubes

2 green bell peppers, chopped

1 large onion, chopped

1 (14.5 oz) can stewed tomatoes

1 cup water

2 (2.5 oz) pkgs Olde Westport Chili Seasoning Mix

1 (12 oz) can beer

1 tsp Olde Westport Ground Jalapeno Pepper, to taste

2 tsp salt

2 (16 oz) cans pinto beans

- Add all ingredients to a 6 qt slow cooker, except beans.
- Stir thoroughly and set temperature on high heat.
- After ½-1 hour, turn slow cooker to low. Stir for the final time.
- Cook for 9-10 hours.
- 30 minutes before serving, drain and rinse the beans under hot water in a colander.
- Add beans to slow cooker and stir.
- To thicken chili, turn temperature to high; leave lid off, and cook 30 minutes.
- Serves 6-8.

Oh! Give me a home where the buffalo roam,
Where the deer and the antelope play.

Upon returning home, he completed another six verses and titled his work "My Western Home."

The words were set to music a year later by Daniel E. Kelly, a carpenter who had moved to the area from Rhode Island. The arrangement proved easy to sing and young people soon made it number one on their "Hit Parade."

In 1947, both houses of the Kansas Legislature passed a bill making "Home on the Range" the official state song.

Higley's restored cabin is located eight miles north, and one mile west, of Athol. It contains one door and one window plus small loft windows at each end of the structure. It is atypical of the period in which it was built in that there is no fireplace, no original stone work nor any wooden floors.

Due to ill health, Higley left Kansas in 1886 seeking a warmer climate. He moved to Arkansas, then to Shawnee, Oklahoma, where he died in 1909 at the age of 86.

Janet and Tom Taggart are proprietors of the Old Bunker Hill Cafe that is housed in a 1916-vintage building. Grain-fed catfish fillets are the specialty of the house. Other fare ranges from center cut top sirloin to boneless chicken breasts and boiled jumbo king crab legs.

Once you're in Bunker Hill, you can't miss the Taggart's cafe. It's about the only business on the main street. Inside, an eclectic mix of furniture includes cabinets from a drug store and an assortment of wooden tables and chairs. The walls are covered with landscape paintings, horns and taxidermied game.

But it's the food that's exceptional. No secret ingredients, though, the recipes are simple.

"We use little seasoning," Tom says. "Quality food doesn't need it."

Cider Stew
"Celebrate! Kansas Food" Contest Winner

2 lbs Stoffle Stew Meat, cut into 1" cubes
3 tbsp vegetable oil
3 tbsp all-purpose flour
¼ tsp crushed thyme
2 tsp Carey Salt
¼ tsp pepper
2 cups Louisburg Cider Mill Apple Cider
2 tbsp vinegar
½ cup water
3 potatoes, peeled and diced
4 Meier's Market Carrots, diced
2 Meier's Market Onions, diced

- In Dutch oven, brown meat in oil.
- Combine flour, thyme, salt and pepper; add to meat.
- Stir in liquids; cook and stir until mixture boils.
- Reduce heat; simmer 1½-2 hours, or until meat is tender.
- Add remaining ingredients; cook 40 minutes, or until vegetables are tender.
- Serves 8.

General Eisenhower's Old-Fashioned Beef Stew
Dwight D. Eisenhower Library, Abilene

4 lbs Nutri-Beef Round Steak, cubed
3 tbsp vegetable oil
10 cups beef stock
2 lbs small Irish potatoes
2 bunches small Polk's Farm Carrots, halved
1½ lbs small Polk's Farm Onions, quartered
4 tomatoes, quartered
1 bunch The Kansas Collection of Carousel Gift Shop Bouquet Garniture of Herbs
¼ cup margarine
¼ cup all-purpose flour
salt, pepper and Accent

- In large saucepan, lightly brown meat in hot oil.
- Add beef stock, vegetables and bouquet garniture.
- When vegetables are done, strain off 2 cups of stock from stew.
- In a 10" skillet, melt margarine.
- Over medium heat, stir in flour. Stirring constantly, cook until bubbly and lightly browned.
- Slowly add reserved stock, salt, pepper and Accent; pour back into stew and simmer for 30 minutes.
- Serves 12.

The Butterfield Overland Despatch ran from Atchison to Denver. It was the idea of David Butterfield who set up a route approximately one hundred miles shorter than the existing trail to the north.

Butterfield obviously was a salesman because he encouraged Eastern investors to spring for six million dollars, a staggering sum in the 1860's.

Indians quickly made the Butterfield Despatch a favorite target. One incident, near Monument Station, involved thirty Cheyennes and a stagecoach. After being attacked, the passengers and driver unhitched the stagecoach and fled on horseback. Instead of pursuing them, the Indians plundered the stagecoach and set fire to it, then did the same to the building at Monument Station.

The Indian menace proved too much for David Butterfield and his financiers and they were forced to shut down approximately eighteen months after beginning operations. Rival Ben Holladay bought the oxen, mules and wagons from the defunct freight line.

Two of the Butterfield Trail's stops were at Russell Springs and Fort Wallace, communities whose populations have dwindled so that there aren't one hundred fifty people between them. Both have small museums commemorating their days in the limelight.

The Butterfield Trail Historical Society Museum at Russell Springs is housed in the former Logan County Courthouse. An 1887 election made the town the county seat over Oakley and two other communities.

Inside the museum are items found at various stations along the Butterfield. There also are artifacts recovered from a nearby encampment of the Negro 10th Cavalry, proposals for a resort lake that was never built, and the story of the Western Nickel and Cobalt Mining Company.

A founder of Western Nickel and Cobalt Mining supposedly found nickel in the hills surrounding Russell Springs and sold stock to finance a mining operation. Money in hand, the promoter went back East under the guise of purchasing equipment, but never returned.

Twice each year Russell Springs overflows with visitors anxious to recapture and experience again some of the customs and celebrations of

SALADS

Winter Wonderland, Riley County

Photo by John L. Schlageck

the Old West. Over Labor Day weekend, crowds gather on Old Settler's Day for a parade, program and basket dinner. Others participate in a contest to see who can throw a favorite fuel of the pioneers the farthest. Since 1975 Russell Springs has officially been the "Cow Chip Capital of Kansas."

The other event, a two-day Butterfield Trail Ride, is held the first weekend in June. Riders travel fifteen to twenty miles the first day and, following breakfast and an outdoor worship service, ride until noon on Sunday. After lunch, a rodeo is held in the local arena.

Old Fort Wallace was abandoned in 1882. All that remains is the old post cemetery, enclosed by stone walls within the Wallace Township Cemetery.

Tombstones, wooden and stone, tell of a time when murder and diseases took their toll.

"John Gates, Admitted to Post Hospital with fractured arm. Arm amputated. Died 1878."

"John McGee, Ireland, Age 38, chronic diarrhea."

"John Etcher, Age 60 from England, froze to death near Wallace, 1877."

"John Larksford, Age 22, Hung by Vigilance Committee at Pond Creek City, 1869."

In a cemetery of approximately fifty graves, there were a lot of unlucky men named John.

Fort Wallace was named in honor of General H.L. Wallace of the Union Army who lost his life in the Civil War Battle of Shiloh. It was once described as ". . . the fightin'est fort in the West!"

The July 27, 1867, issue of *Harpers Weekly* reported that on June 26, a band of three hundred Cheyennes, under the direction of the famous Chief Roman Nose, attacked a stagecoach station two miles from Fort Wallace and ran off with the livestock. Then the Indians advanced

Summer's Special Wheat Fruit Salad

2 cups cooked wheat kernels

¼ cup lemon juice

4 tbsp Sweetheart Honey

2 Rees Fruit Farm Peaches,
peeled and sliced

1 cup blueberries

1 cup sliced Rees Fruit Farm
Strawberries

- Put wheat in bowl; cover and chill.
- Blend lemon juice and honey. Add to wheat and mix well. Chill.
- Before serving, stir in peaches, blueberries and strawberries.
- Makes 8-10 servings.

Fruit Salad with Creamy Cardamom Dressing
"Celebrate! Kansas Food" Contest Winner

1 cup King's Orchard Cantaloupe balls
or cubes

1 cup King's Orchard Watermelon balls
or cubes, seeded

1 cup Moore Orchard Cherries, pitted

1 cup Sargeant Strawberry Farm
Strawberries

1 cup Rees Fruit Farm Blackberries

Creamy Cardamon Dressing:

¾ cup orange juice

1 tbsp cornstarch

¼ tsp cardamom

¼ cup Fowler Honey Farms Honey

1 tbsp Steffen's Butter

1 Sunnyfresh Farms Egg

½ cup whipping cream, whipped

- To make dressing, combine orange juice and cornstarch in small saucepan; blend well.
- Stir in cardamom, honey, butter and egg; mix well.
- Cook over medium heat until thickened, stirring constantly. Cool completely.
- Fold in whipped cream; refrigerate.
- In medium bowl, combine fruits.
- Spoon into glass dishes; refrigerate until serving time.
- Before serving, top with dressing.
- Serves 6-8.

toward the fort when Company G of the 7th U.S. Cavalry, under the command of Captain Barnitz, "went out to meet them and were met by a counter charge that drove them back to the fort with a loss of seven men. Roman Nose was wounded, hit by a sword and shot."

On museum grounds is another reminder of those violent days. You can still see bullet holes in the Pond Creek Station, never plugged after an Indian raid.

The town of Wallace once had a population of 3,500. Fred Harvey, whose food became a staple for railroad passengers, opened his first "Harvey House" restaurant there. Although the Harvey House is gone now, the "Section House," a magnificent native stone structure built by the Union Pacific Railroad as a superintendent's office, still stands there.

F olks in Goodland are a friendly bunch. There's even a Friendly Book Store there. Visitors see a lot of smiling faces, and the greetings are genuine.

Goodland is a commercial center for Northwest Kansas and the westernmost major Kansas community on Interstate 70. The only thing out of the ordinary about the downtown area (other than the fact that businesses open and close an hour later than most of the rest of Kansas, because of a preference for Mountain Standard Time) is the number of "art deco" buildings in the city of 6,000 people.

Webster defines art deco as "a pervasive decorative style of the 1920's and 1930's characterized especially by bold outlines, streamlined and rectilinear forms, and the use of the new materials." The art deco trend was based on two ideas. First, that one needed to distinguish one's period by an art which is original but at the same time speaks for everyone. Second, that one needed to reconcile art with industry.

The Southwestern Bell Telephone Company office cost $125,000 when it was built in 1931. Terra cotta panels and borders on the exterior of the building show Aztec tribal artwork. Although the business office is

Summer Sausage Salad

6 cups fresh spinach, torn in bite-sized pieces, divided

1 small red onion, thinly sliced and halved

1 (16 oz) can garbanzo beans, rinsed and drained

½ (14 oz) stick OhSe Summer Sausage, thinly sliced

⅓ cup Italian salad dressing

- In a salad bowl, layer four cups of torn spinach, onion, beans, sausage, then add remaining two cups of torn spinach.
- To garnish top of salad, cut slices of sausage almost in half, then twist to make cartwheel garnishes.
- Drizzle dressing over salad.
- Serves 4.

Fresh Broccoli Salad

1 large bunch broccoli, coarsely chopped

6 slices Ernie's Hickory Smoked Bacon, fried crisp and crumbled

1 cup raisins

½ cup chopped red onion

1 Harvest House Cucumber, diced

Dressing:

½ cup mayonnaise

½ tsp celery seed

2 tbsp sugar

1 tbsp vinegar

Garnish:

1 (8 oz) pkg Emogene's Soy Goodies Soy Nuts

- Combine salad ingredients; set aside.
- Combine dressing ingredients and blend well.
- Combine dressing with salad ingredients; stir until well mixed.
- Let marinate in the refrigerator 1-3 hours.
- Garnish with desired amount of soy nuts just before serving.
- Serves 6-8.

now closed, the structure's inner beauty remains. The ceiling is heavily beamed with telephone poles trimmed and decorated in Indian patterns. The business counter is supported by hand-carved totem poles which are accurate replicas of artifacts. The distinct Indian motif incorporates symbols taken from decorations on silver, pottery, blankets and baskets. Each has a meaning, and whole stories can be told by combining the designs.

Another beautiful example of art deco is the Sherman County Courthouse. Also built in 1931, its design ideals resemble the telephone company building.

The High Plains Museum isn't art deco, it's just a modern brick structure. Inside are seven talking dioramas of the surrounding area. A 1902 Holsman auto is one rare item on display. The museum's main exhibit tells the tale of two local men's early quest to free themselves from earth's gravity.

Six years after the Wright brothers made their famous flight at Kitty Hawk, North Carolina, two Rock Island Railroad machinists in Goodland, Kansas, decided to take to the air. William J. Purvis and Charles A. Wilson began building what they hoped would become the Purvis-Wilson Flying Machine.

Theirs was a strange looking "bird" . . . twin sets of blades attached to a long central shaft, and no wings. It was a helicopter. But, even without the two seven-horsepower engines, the machine weighed four hundred pounds, too heavy to stay airborne.

The first flight was less than a success. History maintains that the craft's frame-mounted Curtiss engines weighed too much. During the flight a guy wire broke and the machine crashed.

An onlooker's version of this story is much more colorful. "The craft rose with the grace of a 'crippled praying mantis' and a sudden gust of wind propelled it into the water tower destroying the tower and the

Confetti Asparagus Toss

1 lb fresh Bauman Farms Asparagus, cut in 2" pieces

1 small head G H Farms Lettuce, torn in bite-size pieces

1 cup sliced celery

¼ cup sliced green onions and tops

½ cup vegetable oil

2 tbsp white wine vinegar

2 tbsp lemon juice

¼ cup finely chopped cooked beets

1 hard cooked egg, finely chopped

1 tbsp snipped David's Herbs Parsley

1 tsp paprika

1 tsp sugar

1 tsp salt

½ tsp dry mustard

4 drops hot pepper sauce

- Cook asparagus until tender; drain. Chill.
- Combine with lettuce, celery and onion.
- For dressing, combine remaining ingredients in jar; cover and shake well.
- Pour dressing over salad; toss lightly.
- Serves 6-8.

Cauliflower Salad

1 small head Coltrain Vegetables Cauliflower, cut into flowerets

1 cup chopped celery

1 (10 oz) pkg frozen peas, cooked and chilled

¼ cup chopped onion

1½ tsp salt

⅛ tsp pepper

¾ cup mayonnaise

- Combine all ingredients.
- Chill.
- Serves 8.

flying machine."

Either version of the aircraft's demise was enough to discourage stockholders in Purvis' and Wilson's Goodland Aviation Company. Although a patent was applied for on March 18, 1910, the craft never flew again.

All that remains of America's first patented helicopter are two rusted pieces on either side of a mockup at the High Plains Museum in Goodland. The replica doesn't fly but the blades turn when you push a button.

Among Goodland's annual events are the Northwest Kansas District Free Fair and Tri-State Farm Show in July, windwagon races in October, and a June air show at Renner Field.

A dining experience at Dave Haug's Smith Center Ingleboro restaurant is more than just a meal. The setting, the food, and the service allows one to slip back into a more peaceful, unhurried era, when everyone had time to enjoy the good life.

Haug's restaurant is billed "dining at its best in opulent Victorian splendor." It has become a must for Kansas gourmets. Alaskan king crab and other seafoods are complemented by quality prime rib and steaks. However, those who enjoy "down home" cooking aren't left out. There's fried chicken, catfish and shrimp on the menu. All rolls are baked on premise and soups and salad dressings are made from scratch.

Ingleboro is named after J.R. Burrows, builder of the Victorian-style house it now occupies, and his wife, whose maiden name was Ingles. Burrows, who moved to Smith Center in the early 1880's, founded the Smith Center National Bank. He later served as Kansas' Secretary of State.

The Burrows' Ingleboro home covered a city block and had a private park complete with deer, a stream and a gazebo.

For many years Burrows was asked by his friend Henry Williams just how much he would take for the house. Burrows would always laugh and

Marinated Mushrooms

1 lb whole fresh Toto Cure of Kansas
Mushrooms, cleaned and trimmed

1 small onion, thinly sliced

¼ cup chopped green pepper

1 tbsp chopped pimento (optional)

1 (8 oz) btl Italian dressing

salad greens

- Put mushrooms in container with lid.
- Add onions, green pepper, pimento and dressing. Stir to coat each mushroom with dressing.
- Marinate 2-4 hours or overnight.
- Remove from marinade to serve.
- Serve on a bed of salad greens.

Marinated Mushroom Salad

½ cup chopped fresh onion

¼ cup chopped celery

½ cup sour cream

¼ cup mayonnaise

2 tbsp fresh lemon juice

1 tbsp chopped fresh Sunflower Organic
Farm Parsley

1 tsp horseradish

1 tsp prepared mustard

1 tsp salt

¼ tsp dried leaf oregano

⅛ tsp pepper

1 lb fresh Toto Cure of Kansas
Mushrooms, thinly sliced

G-H Farms Lettuce

- For dressing, mix together all ingredients except mushrooms and lettuce.
- Place mushrooms in bowl; add dressing and mix well.
- Chill at least 2 hours.
- Serve on lettuce.
- Serves 6-8.

tell him "it's not for sale." Then one day, to end Williams' offers, Burrows decided to call his bluff. He told Williams that he could buy Ingleboro for a sum Burrows thought was so astronomical it would be out of the question. Without batting an eye, Williams said "sold." Burrows, taken aback, attempted to regain his property for one thousand dollars . . . that's how much a person's word meant then.

Williams refused to let Burrows renege on his verbal agreement.

Years later the home was turned into a hospital (most of the babies born in Smith Center in the early 1940's were delivered in an upstairs bedroom). In 1952, it became a nursing home. Now it is a truly unique dining experience.

What do Horace Greeley, Henry Clay, Samuel Jones Tilden and "Old Fuss and Feathers" have in common? They were all unsuccessful presidential candidates featured in the Gallery of Also Rans on the mezzanine of the First State Bank in Norton.

Greeley, a newspaperman who popularized the phrase, "go West, young man," reportedly spent a stopover at Stage Station 15, in Norton, with the likes of Pat Garrett, Roy Bean and the parents of Billy the Kid. It was in the building that houses the replica station that the local bank president came up with the idea for the gallery.

If you're wondering who "Old Fuss and Feathers" was, General Winfield Scott is his real name. And Henry Clay? He lost the presidency three times, with three different parties: Democratic, National Republican and Whig.

Samuel Tilden lost the presidential race by only one electoral vote. He actually received two hundred fifty-thousand more votes than his opponent. However, the Electoral Commission declared Rutherford Birchard Hayes the winner.

NORTHEAST KANSAS

Northeast Kansas is one of the state's most scenic regions. It consists of uplands, hills and, in the extreme northeast, a glaciated area. It is Kansas' "Lake Country." Nine major reservoirs and more than thirty municipal and state lakes provide excellent water recreation for residents and visitors alike.

Many Northeast Kansas attractions played major roles in the opening of the West. The Hollenberg Pony Express Station at Hanover is the lone remaining original, unaltered building from the days of the short-lived but famous mail service. Brookville, where the local hotel is famous for its chicken dinners, was a major shipping point for cattle driven up from Texas.

Today Northeast Kansas is a mixture of rural and metropolitan— farmers, ranchers and blue and white collar workers. It is a major distribution center for national and international commerce and, as it has always been, the seat of government for a people who have truly

Marinated Fresh Vegetable Salad

*1 cup thinly sliced J. C. Meier & Sons
Cucumber*

*1 cup thinly sliced J. C. Meier & Sons
Squash*

*1 cup thinly sliced J. C. Meier & Sons
Carrots*

1 cup chopped celery

*1 medium onion, sliced and separated
into rings*

¾ cup sugar

1 cup vinegar

½ cup vegetable oil

1 tsp celery seeds

1 tsp Carey Salt

½ tsp pepper

- Combine cucumber, squash, carrots, celery and onion in large bowl.
- In a screw-top jar or blender, combine sugar, vinegar, oil, celery seeds, salt and pepper. Cover and shake to mix.
- Pour over vegetables.
- Cover bowl and refrigerate 4 hours or overnight.
- Keeps well in refrigerator for several days.
- Serves 8.

Asparagus Pasta Salad

*¾ lb Pendleton's Fresh Asparagus,
bias-sliced into 1" pieces*

½ cup pitted ripe olives, sliced

*12 Meier's Market Cherry Tomatoes,
quartered*

3 tbsp snipped Pickett's Gardens Parsley

¼ cup vinegar

3 tbsp olive or vegetable oil

1 clove garlic, minced

1 tsp dried oregano, crushed

½ tsp dried marjoram, crushed

½ tsp salt

dash pepper

4 oz Pasta Mills Fettucine or Spaghetti

- Cook fresh asparagus and drain well.
- In mixing bowl, combine asparagus, olives, tomatoes and parsley.
- In a screw-top jar, combine vinegar, oil, garlic, oregano, marjoram, salt and pepper; cover and shake.
- Pour dressing over asparagus mixture; cover and chill.
- Cook pasta according to pkg directions.
- Drain; rinse with cold water, then drain again.
- Continue rinsing and draining until pasta is thoroughly chilled.
- Turn into salad bowl.
- Spoon vegetables and dressing on top; toss well.
- Serves 6.

Hearty Reuben Supper Salad

4 Britt's Garden Acres Potatoes

1 (10 oz) pkg green peas with pearl onions

1 (8 oz) can sauerkraut, rinsed and drained

¾ cup diced celery

½ cup shredded Swiss cheese

1 cup mayonnaise

2 tbsp Grandma's Homestyle Mustard

1 tsp crushed caraway

½ tsp garlic salt

⅛ tsp pepper

12-16 slices cooked Hiawatha Corned Beef

- Cook potatoes, dice and set aside.
- Cook green peas as directed on pkg, omitting butter and increasing water to 3 tbsp; drain.
- In large bowl, combine peas, potatoes, sauerkraut, celery and cheese; toss lightly to mix.
- In small bowl, combine mayonnaise, mustard, caraway, garlic salt and pepper; mix well.
- Add to potato mixture; mix gently.
- Chill about 2 hours.
- Spoon salad in center of serving platter and arrange corned beef around it.
- Serves 6-8.

Lemon Lite Seafood Salad

1 (5 oz) pkg Soup Lady Pasta Soup Mix

1 (16 oz) can black olives, pitted

1 cup chopped celery

1 (6 oz) ctn lowfat lemon yogurt

1 cup mayonnaise

1 (8 oz) pkg cooked seafood (shrimp, crab, etc.)

shredded lettuce

- Cook soup mix according to #1 directions except drain.
- Combine all remaining ingredients and mix well.
- Chill several hours or overnight.
- Serve plain or on a bed of finely shredded lettuce.
- Serves 4.

experienced reaching "To the Stars Through Difficulties" (The State Motto: "Ad Astra per Aspera").

Situated high on bluffs overlooking the wide Missouri River, Fort Leavenworth looks more like a college campus than a military post. No sentries stand guard outside perimeters of barbed wire, timber or stone. Instead, its entrance is a tree-lined drive beside an eighteen-hole golf course, grassy fields and large ponds. The officers' living quarters are mostly Victorian-style homes with manicured lawns.

Dwight D. Eisenhower, Douglas MacArthur, George S. Patton, William "Billy" Mitchell, George C. Marshall and George Armstrong Custer served at this, the oldest, continuously garrisoned military installation west of the Mississippi. Although they're gone now, other heroes whose fame was fleeting, remain in Fort Leavenworth National Cemetery. They include four officers of the Seventh Cavalry Regiment who were killed at the most famous battle of the Indian wars, the Little Bighorn.

Ironically, two of the deceased heroes were related to Custer, the regiment's commander. Captain James Calhoun was his brother-in-law and Captain Thomas W. Custer was his brother. Although virtually ignored by historians, Tom was twice awarded the Congressional Medal of Honor for separate engagements during the Civil War when he daringly crossed enemy lines and captured Confederate flags in the midst of raging battles.

Fort Leavenworth is a registered National Historical Landmark and much of its more than five thousand acres is accessible to civilians. You can drive through secluded woods, hike nature trails over rolling hills, or walk to the many sites listed in a self-guided tour booklet available at the post museum. Be sure to notice the mystery surrounding the wall plaques at guidepoint number seven on the tour. One plaque on the stone wall indicates that the wall was part of the fort's original fortifications.

South-of-the-Border Grilled Chicken Salad
"Celebrate! Kansas Food" Contest Winner

¼ cup soy sauce

¼ cup water

1 lime, juiced

⅛ tsp garlic powder

1 tsp freshly ground pepper, divided

1 lb skinless, boneless chicken breasts

8 cups torn Merritt Horticultural Center Lettuce

½ cup grated G-H Farms Cucumber

¾ cup The Whole Enchilada's Mexican Salsa

¼ cup cucumber salad dressing

1 G-H Farms Green Pepper, sliced into thin rings

2 green onions, thinly sliced

2 tomatoes, cut into wedges

fresh parsley sprigs

3 green onion tops, chopped

Glazed Pecans:

1 cup Carden Pecans, halved

¼ cup sugar

2 tbsp water

¼ tsp Carey Salt

- Mix soy sauce, water, lime juice, garlic powder and ½ tsp pepper.
- Add chicken and marinate in refrigerator 6-24 hours.
- Grill chicken over charcoal just until done, but not dry.
- Slice diagonally into 2″ strips and season with remaining pepper.
- Chill until serving time.
- For glazed pecans combine pecans, sugar, water and salt in small saucepan.
- Cook over medium high heat, 5-10 minutes, stirring constantly until syrup has changed to crystals and pecans are evenly coated.
- Spread on cookie sheet and bake in 225 degree oven for 45 minutes-1 hour.
- To assemble salad on a large platter, layer in this order: lettuce, grated cucumber, salsa, dressing, chicken, green pepper rings, green onion slices and glazed pecans.
- Garnish with tomato wedges, fresh parsley sprigs and green onion tops.
- Serves 4.

Colorful Cole Slaw

½ head of cabbage, shredded

1 large Bismarck Gardens Carrot, peeled and grated

1 cup raisins

Dressing:

creamy cucumber dressing

1 (8 oz) pkg Emogene's Soy Goodies Soy Nuts

- Combine cabbage, carrots and raisins; mix well. Refrigerate, covered.
- Just before serving, add desired amount of dressing.
- Garnish with soy nuts.
- Serves 4.

The other states there never was a stone wall around the fort. Whatever its origin, the wall as it exists today was restored in the early part of this century by the Daughter's of the American Revolution.

The Fort Leavenworth museum is also part of the tour. It contains an outstanding collection of horse-drawn carriages including one that Abraham Lincoln used while visiting the post. Other displays portray more than a century of Army history and, as the fort's theme goes, "Fort Leavenworth's Role in Westward Expansion."

As might be expected, many characters have approached the one hundred sixty-year old fort claiming to have invented war machines that would revolutionize the military. Today, would-be inventors test their products before giving public demonstrations. Not back then!

For example, "Windwagon" Thomas claimed his wagon would move briskly across the plains using only wind power. To harness the Kansas breezes he attached a single sheet of canvas to a seven-foot mast. Any barnyard engineer would have scoffed at his idea knowing that the twenty-five-foot long wooden vehicle, with four, twelve-foot wheels, was too heavy to be budged by such a small sail. Still, Windwagon attracted many investors in his get-rich-quick scheme.

On a day when it was hard to stand erect in the Kansas wind, Thomas readied to set sail. The brake was released and . . . nothing happened.

Thomas' failure necessitated he make a hasty exit from the demonstration, and as imagined, his former partners were in close pursuit.

Another such inventor had an idea for a mobile artillery piece, a muzzle-loading cannon strapped to the back of a pack mule. A large crowd gathered for a demonstration of this weapon of the future. The unfortunate animal was positioned in the opposite direction from the on-lookers but, when the fuse was lit, it turned around to see what was going on. With the cannon now pointed directly at them, the spectators scattered.

"Boom!"

SANDWICHES

Festive autumn field, Doniphan County

Photo by Loreen Locke McMillan

Miraculously everyone escaped injury but the mule. It was last seen tumbling down the embankment and into the river, never to surface again.

The city of Leavenworth, adjacent to the fort, is the oldest organized community in Kansas. Buffalo Bill Cody called it home, moving there in 1854 at the age of 9. When he turned 13 he went to work for locally-owned Russell, Major and Waddell Freight Line and later became a Pony Express rider for the same company. The King of the Wild West is remembered every third week in September during Leavenworth's largest annual celebration, "Buffalo Bill Days."

Robert Stroud, "The Birdman of Alcatraz," and Al Capone spent some time in Leavenworth, literally. The criminals had cells in the federal penitentiary known as the Big House. You can drive by the prison and take pictures from your moving car, but guards frown at anyone who stops to "shoot."

Leavenworth has many impressive nineteenth century buildings, one of which is the Leavenworth County Historical Museum's Carroll House. This Victorian mansion, built in 1867, contains exquisitely crafted wood carvings in its foyer, library, parlor and dining rooms. Beautiful, ornate stained glass windows, and heirloom quality antiques add to its elegance. Guided tours last forty-five minutes.

Another Leavenworth building, Immanuel Chapel, was featured in *Ripley's Believe It Or Not*. The Chapel's unique architecture is reminiscent of the early European cathedrals.

The streets of downtown Lawrence are lively today. Boutiques, stores and art galleries do a booming business, no mall has taken the shoppers away. There's ample free parking, fine cafes and

Basil Beef Pockets

1 lb boneless Hoseney's Beef Top Round Steak

½ cup soy sauce

2 tbsp red wine vinegar

2 cloves garlic, minced

2 tsp dried basil flakes

2 medium carrots, thinly sliced

1 yellow bell pepper, cut into ¼" x 1" strips

2 cups small broccoli flowerets

2 tbsp vegetable oil, divided

½ small onion, thinly sliced

10 large Toto Cure of Kansas Mushrooms

¼ cup cold water

2 tsp cornstarch

3 medium Roma tomatoes, cut into ½" cubes

4, 6" N & J Pita Bakery Pita Bread Rounds, sliced in half

leaf lettuce, tomato, fresh basil sprigs to garnish

- Thinly slice beef round steak into bite-size strips.
- Mix together soy sauce, vinegar, garlic and basil.
- In non-metal container, combine beef and marinade.
- Refrigerate several hours or overnight, turning occasionally.
- Spray a wok or large skillet with non-stick spray coating.
- Heat wok over medium heat.
- Add carrots, bell pepper and broccoli; stir-fry 5 minutes.
- Add 1 tbsp oil, onions and mushrooms, stir-fry another 5 minutes.
- Remove vegetables and set aside.
- Drain beef; reserve ¼ cup marinade.
- Place remaining oil in wok and heat.
- Add beef strips and stir-fry in hot oil 5 minutes, or until desired doneness.
- Mix water, reserved marinade and cornstarch together in small bowl.
- Add to meat mixture in wok.
- Cook until bubbly, stirring constantly.
- Return vegetables to wok and add tomatoes, cooking until thoroughly heated.
- Spoon mixture into warmed pita bread rounds.
- To serve, place beef pockets on lettuce-lined platter.
- Garnish with tomato and basil sprigs; serve immediately.
- Serves 4.

restaurants, and Free State beer from the only micro-brewery in Kansas. The area's buildings have nineteenth century charm and proud owners who keep them in mint condition. It's difficult to believe that several times in its history, men have laid Lawrence in ruin.

William Quantrill and his Confederate raiders ravaged Lawrence during the Civil War. The orders he gave his band of cutthroats were to "Kill every man and burn every house." When they left, nearly one hundred fifty men had been killed and much of the town was in flames.

Hannah Oliver, a small child then, later recalled the events.

"My mother saw a fearful sight. She saw a troop of guerrillas ride up to the Griswold gate. She saw the four men who lived in Griswold's house come out at the front door, pass through the gate, and then start in single file toward the town. Then she heard the shots of the guerrillas and saw the men fall, in the same order in which they had been walking.

"The four men lay in the fierce heat of the sun and of the burning houses. A little later, another posse rode up and shot at the fallen men again. When the departure of the enemy made it possible to go to them, Dr. Griswold and Mr. Trask were dead. Mr. Thorpe suffered great agony and died the next day. Mr. Baker, severely wounded, slowly recovered."

Oliver continued that after "The outlaws left town . . . the scene was beyond description: smoke rising from hundreds of burning buildings, the dead lying in the streets and dooryards, women and children searching for husbands and fathers, friend seeking friend."

This was the second time in nine years that Lawrence had been devastated. Earlier, Sam Jones had been the culprit.

Jones was a sheriff, a pro-slavery sheriff at that. He had once arrested a Free-State man for making threats. The crime? Complaining about a murder committed by a pro-slavery man.

After the arrest, the sheriff and his posse were met by fifteen men, south of Lawrence, who rescued the prisoner. Jones used the incident as an excuse to prepare for an attack on the city. Soon one thousand five hundred men were ready to fight with him.

B-Q Burgers

1 lb Quinter Meat Ground Beef
1 lb ground turkey
½ cup seasoned bread crumbs
1 (8 oz) btl Bob'S B-Q Sauce
1 cup grated Alma Cheddar Cheese
lettuce, tomatoes, sliced pickles
to garnish

- In bowl, combine ground beef, ground turkey, bread crumbs and sauce.
- Form into patties.
- Grill over medium hot coals until done.
- Top with grated cheese.
- Add lettuce, tomatoes, pickles and more sauce to taste.
- Serves 6-8.

Deli Flip

1, 9" frozen pie crust
1 cup sauerkraut, rinsed and drained
¼ cup thousand island dressing
1 tsp lime or lemon juice
¼ lb Swift Premium® Honey Loaf, thinly sliced
¼ lb Swiss cheese
¼ lb Swift Premium® Hard Salami, thinly sliced
1 Sunnyfresh Farms Egg
1 tbsp water

- Preheat oven to 400 degrees.
- Remove wrapper and foil pan from frozen pie crust.
- Place crust on greased cookie sheet and let thaw 10 minutes at room temperature.
- Combine sauerkraut, dressing and lemon juice.
- Layer honey loaf, cheese, sauerkraut mixture and salami on half of pie crust.
- Fold remaining half of crust over layered meat mixture.
- Press edge of crust together with fork.
- Pierce top of crust with fork.
- Beat egg with water.
- Brush over top and sides of crust.
- Bake in oven for 20 minutes.
- Cut into wedges.
- Serves 4.

One afternoon the sheriff and his force entered the town with five pieces of artillery. They attacked the newspaper office and torched the Free State Hotel. As the walls caved, in Sheriff Jones shouted, "This is the happiest moment of my life."

The hotel in ruins, Jones' men robbed stores and ransacked and pillaged houses. In their final act they burned the territorial governor's house.

The two tragedies didn't break the spirit of the citizens of Lawrence. As the editor of the *Kansas Weekly Tribune* wrote later, after the Quantrill raid: "Lawrence is not to 'wink out.' We have a glorious record and a destiny. We are to be one of the largest cities west of the Missouri. There is no possibility of mistaking that . . . Our town will not be like a ruffian hole destroyed. It will rise from its ashes in a space of time which will astonish even Quantrill himself."

As prophesied, Lawrence rose from the ashes. It has never become one of the larger cities west of the Missouri River but it is a vibrant, vital city just the same.

Lawrence is home to The University of Kansas which spread out from Mount Oread, where Sheriff Jones gathered his horsemen. Not only is the city recognized as one of America's top institutions for higher learning, it has a pretty good basketball team as well. The "Jayhawks" were 1988 men's National Collegiate Athletic Association champions.

The Helen Forseman Spencer Museum of Art, on campus, is one of the finest university art museums in the United States. More than 25,000 objects are in the collection, including paintings by the masters, and important sculptures by Soldani, Emile Hebert, Augustus Saint-Gaudens and Frederic Remington.

The university's Museum of Anthropology presents collections of ethnographic art from cultures around the world. The museum, in conjunction with local Haskell Indian Junior College, presents an art show and Indian Market each fall.

Fossils and mammals are exhibited at KU's Museum of Natural

Hearty Ham Healthwich

1 (10 oz) pkg frozen chopped broccoli,
cooked and drained

½ cup chopped celery

¼ cup chopped green pepper

¼ cup chopped onion

1 hard cooked egg, chopped

¼ tsp salt

⅛ tsp pepper

½ pkg ranch style dressing mix

1 (8 oz) ctn plain yogurt

12 thin slices Pony Express Ranch Ham

1 medium tomato, cut into 8 slices

4 slices thin sliced whole wheat bread

- Combine vegetables, egg, salt and pepper.
- Combine dressing mix and yogurt.
- Toss vegetables with ½ cup dressing. Chill remaining dressing.
- Place 2 rounded tbsp of vegetables on each ham slice; roll up.
- Arrange 2 tomato slices on each bread slice; top with 3 ham rolls and 1 tbsp chilled dressing. Pass remaining dressing.
- Serves 4.

Back to School Sandwich

1 cup chopped, cooked chicken

6 slices Lone Pine Farms Bacon,
chopped

½ cup chopped apple

¼ cup chopped water chestnuts

2 tbsp chopped green pepper

2 tbsp minced onion

⅓ cup creamy cucumber salad dressing

2 tsp lemon juice

6 lettuce leaves

6, 6" N & J Bakery Pita Bread Rounds,
sliced in half

- Measure chicken into bowl.
- Fry bacon until crisp.
- Drain and add to chicken along with apple, water chestnuts, green pepper and onion.
- Mix lightly until well blended.
- Add salad dressing and lemon juice; mix well.
- Place lettuce in pita pockets; fill with chicken mixture.
- Serves 6.

Fort Scott National Historic Site, Fort Scott

Hickory Joes

1 lb ground beef
½ cup finely chopped onion
2 tbsp chopped green pepper
salt and pepper
1 cup Curley's Hickory Barbecue Sauce
Rainbo Hamburger Buns

- Saute ground beef with onion and green pepper; drain grease off.
- Salt and pepper to taste; add sauce to mixture; simmer 10-15 minutes.
- Spoon on a bun.
- Serves 4-6.

Sunny Roast Beef Sandwich

2 slices "SunnyWheat" Bread
1 tbsp hot mustard sauce
1 slice American cheese
1 oz thinly sliced Galey's Roast Beef
⅛ cup R. B. Rice Coleslaw
2 tomato slices

- Spread the bread with hot mustard sauce.
- Top 1 slice with cheese, roast beef, coleslaw and tomatoes.
- Top with other slice of bread.
- Serves 1.

Hot & Hearty Ham & Cheese

2 tbsp butter or margarine, softened
2 tbsp chopped onion
2 tbsp prepared Grandma's Homestyle Mustard
1 tbsp sesame seeds
dash Worcestershire sauce
4 whole wheat hamburger buns
8 slices OhSe Ham
4 slices Swiss cheese

- Combine first 5 ingredients in small mixing bowl; mix well.
- Spread mixture on buns.
- Place 2 slices ham and 1 slice Swiss cheese on bottom half of each bun.
- Cover with bun tops.
- Wrap each sandwich in aluminum foil and heat in 325 degree oven for 10-15 minutes.
- Serves 4.

History. Visitors are impressed by its mounted animals in dioramas and other exhibits. The museum's most famous resident is Comanche, the only animal of Custer's Seventh Calvary that wasn't killed or captured by the Indians on the Little Bighorn battlefield.

Comanche, the horse of Captain Myles W. Keogh, got his name as the result of a wound it received during an earlier skirmish. A soldier told Keough that he had seen an arrow strike the animal's hindquarters and, when it did, the horse yelled like a Comanche.

Following the Little Bighorn battle, the wounded Comanche was nursed back to health . . . "his kind treatment and comfort should be a special pride and solicitude on the part of the Seventh Cavalry, to the end that his life may be prolonged to the utmost limit," General Orders No. 7 read. "Wounded and scarred as he is, his very silence speaks more eloquently than words, of the desperate struggle against overwhelming numbers, of the hopeless conflict and of the heroic manner in which all went down on that fatal day."

Comanche retired to Fort Riley, Kansas, and when he died the officers of the Seventh Cavalry wanted to preserve him. L.L. Dyche of the University of Kansas agreed to taxidermy him for four hundred dollars. Later, in a letter to the officers, Dyche agreed to waive his fee if Comanche would be left at the University. He's been there since.

Johnson County is affluent, trendy, suburban. It is one of Kansas City's "in" places to live, only minutes via interstate highway from the city's downtown core. Residents of Leawood, Fairway, Mission Hills and other communities there, keep area Cadillac, BMW and Mercedes-Benz auto dealerships prospering. Shopping centers are plentiful.

Some of Greater Kansas City's finest restaurants are in Johnson County. Overland Park, Kansas' fourth largest city and Johnson County's center of commerce, has more than one hundred restaurants featuring cuisines from Chinese and Mexican to the delicious barbecue

Mexican Puffed Sandwiches

1¼ cups The Wheat Bin Kwik Mix

¼ cup mayonnaise

1 egg

2 cups shredded cheese (Monterey Jack, hot pepper, Cheddar, etc.)

2 tbsp Rabbit Creek Spicey Mexican Dip Mix

6 slices bread

- Mix first 3 ingredients together.
- Stir in cheese and dip mix.
- Spread mixture over bread.
- Bake on ungreased cookie sheet in 450 degree oven for 10 minutes.
- Serves 6.

Cheesy Chili English Muffins

1 pkg Dad's Favorite Chili Mix

½ lb Alma Cheddar Cheese, grated

½ lb Monterey Jack Cheese, grated

1 pkg English muffins, split

chopped jalapeno peppers (optional)

- Prepare chili mix according to pkg directions.
- Preheat oven at broiler setting with rack in the center.
- Mix together the 2 cheeses.
- Place opened muffins on baking sheet, opened side up.
- Toast under broiler until lightly toasted.
- Meanwhile, heat prepared chili mix.
- Remove toasted muffins from oven and cover each muffin with a heaping ladle full of chili.
- Sprinkle each chili-topped muffin with a handful of the cheese mixture. Add jalapenos at this time, if desired.
- Return to oven and broil until cheese is melted.
- Serves 12.

Kansas City is noted for. Hotels are less than a half hour drive from the Kansas City Royals baseball park, Kansas City Chiefs football stadium, Worlds of Fun theme park, and virtually any other major Kansas City attraction.

A recent Overland Park arrival is the National Collegiate Athletic Association (NCAA) headquarters. The first floor of its new seven-story building contains a Visitors Center featuring the great moments in intercollegiate athletics for the twenty-one sports and seventy-seven national championships that the association administers. Student athletes, member institutions, and nationally recognized individuals who have achieved success in both their athletic and business careers, also are recognized at the center. In addition, a multi-purpose theater shows videos on a variety of sports, and a gift shop sells NCAA championship merchandise.

Two special Overland Park attractions for the young, and the young at heart, are the Deanna Rose Memorial Farmstead and the Theatre for Young America. At the Farmstead, children can pet horses, cows, sheep, goats and other farm animals. The Theatre features professional actors performing plays for children.

Old Shawnee Town, in neighboring Shawnee, has the look of a pioneer community one hundred years ago. The complex includes many original buildings dating back to the mid and late 1800's.

Shawnee Methodist Mission in Fairway, established in 1830, became a school where Indian children of many tribes learned manual arts, English and agriculture. Today it is operated by the Kansas State Historical Society.

A popular Johnson County event is the Kansas State Barbecue Championship in Lenxa's Sar-Ko-Par Park each June. More than forty-thousand persons are attracted to the one-day competition by free admission, free food samples, and plenty of shared recipes and barbecuing hints.

Adjacent to Johnson County is Kansas City, Kansas, the "City of Festivals." More than two dozen such events are held here each year.

SAUCES

The Flint Hills, part of the nation's largest remaining natural prairie

Several outstanding tourist attractions can be found in Kansas City and surrounding Wyandotte County. The Woodlands is a twin-track facility where America's finest greyhounds and horses race. Even if you're not a bettor, you must experience dining in the Clubhouse. The chefs are superb, many having come from some of Kansas City's finest restaurants. The prices, on the other hand, are much lower than you would pay at such establishments.

The *America* and *Missouri River Queen* excursion boats regularly ply the Missouri River from their dock at "River City, U.S.A." in the Fairfax district. They provide a relaxing way to see Kansas and Missouri from another perspective, while being entertained, and while enjoying a scrumptious prime rib buffet.

Relive yesteryear at the beautiful Granada Theatre on Minnesota Street. It's the last operating movie palace in the Kansas City area and a treat for those of us who can remember them, as well as the younger generation accustomed to crackerbox-sized cinemas at malls.

The Granada's architecture is Spanish-Mediterranean. Its unique Boler Atmospheric Ceiling gives a sensation of being out-of-doors. "Stars" twinkle overhead, occasionally disappearing from view, hidden by clouds traveling from horizon to horizon. The illusion is a good one, created by two film projectors.

The Granada's Grande Barton Theatre Pipe Organ was originally located in the Paramount Theatre in Newport News, Virginia. It has over two thousand tuned percussions and speaking pipes that lend accompaniment to the silent movies it shows with such sounds as door bells, telephones, sirens and drums. The best place to experience the sound is from the center section, balcony.

Kansas City's National Agricultural Center and Hall of Fame includes America's largest and most varied collection of agricultural artifacts. The Renaissance Festival, one of the city's most popular events, is held on adjacent grounds. The medieval theme fair begins Labor Day weekend and continues every weekend thereafter until mid-October. Turkey drumsticks, baklava, old-fashioned fritters and other good food is

Honey Mustard Dill Dressing

4 tbsp red wine vinegar
4 tsp Dijon mustard
4 tsp Yellow Brick Road Honey
¼ tsp salt
¼ tsp pepper
¾ cup olive oil
2 tsp Prairie Bounty Dill Seed

- Whisk together vinegar, mustard, honey, salt and pepper.
- Gradually pour in olive oil, whisking constantly until thick.
- Add dill seed.
- Let flavors blend 1 hour.
- Makes 1 cup.

Raspberry BBQ Vinaigrette Dressing

1 (12 oz) btl Flower of the Flames Raspberry BBQ Sauce
6 tbsp olive oil
8 tbsp Briarwood Farms Raspberry Vinegar

- Combine all ingredients in a bowl; mix well.
- Chill and serve with tossed green salad or salad with grilled chicken strips.
- Makes 2½ cups.

Buttered Barbecue Sauce

¼ cup butter
¼ cup chopped onion
1 cup Curley's Mesquite Barbecue Sauce
4 tsp fresh lemon juice
1 tbsp Worcestershire sauce
1 tbsp firmly packed brown sugar
½ tsp dry mustard
⅛ tsp Carey Salt

- Melt butter in a small saucepan; saute onion until tender.
- Add remaining ingredients; mix well.
- Simmer, uncovered, 10 minutes.
- Makes 1½ cups.

served. Try my favorite dessert, a Renaissance Sundae—vanilla ice cream covered with sliced bananas, honey and sunflower seeds.

At least once a year I hop a train to "Nowhere." Usually it's the third weekend in October when nearby Baldwin city holds its Maple Leaf Festival.

Nowhere is an hour's drive from Kansas City, then a short ride from Baldwin City's historic depot on the Midland Railroad. Nowhere is really nothing more than a sign, planted in Douglas County farmland, but the setting is lovely.

When the train reaches Nowhere it's gone about as far as it can go. The Midland Railroad locomotive switches from being a pusher to a puller and heads back to the train station. The forty-five minute round-trip covers just a fraction of the many miles its predecessor, the Leavenworth, Lawrence and Fort Gibson Railroad, once ran over the same right of way.

James Lane was the LL&FG's first president and chief promoter. He announced to anyone who would listen that his would be the best railroad around. The more he talked the farther the tracks began to stretch. "Fort Gibson will only be a temporary stop," he proclaimed of the Indian Territory (later Oklahoma) outpost. "Why, we'll go all the way to Galveston on the Gulf of Mexico!"

At the time Lane was also a United States Senator, and thus was able to acquire U.S. government money to fund his railroad—one of four original right-of-ways in Kansas.

As every politician knows, in order to make money you have to spend money, preferably someone else's. Lane approached the voters of Douglas and Franklin counties and secured five hundred thousands dollars in bonds to build his dream. Since the value of the bonds was estimated to be only half of their face value, he convinced the state to guarantee to bring them up to their full value.

Herbed Vinaigrette Dressing

½ cup cider vinegar

½ tsp salt

¼ tsp garlic salt

¼ tsp black pepper

1 cup olive oil

1 tsp finely chopped, fresh Merritt Horticultural Center Chives

1 tsp finely chopped, fresh Merritt Horticultural Center Thyme or Dill

1 tsp finely chopped, fresh Merritt Horticultural Center Italian Flat-Leaf Parsley

- Vigorously mix ingredients together.
- Makes 1½ cups.

Sweet and Sour Sauce

2 tbsp cornstarch

⅛ tsp ginger

1 clove garlic, minced

1 (10.75 oz) can condensed chicken broth

⅓ cup Golden Mill Sorghum

⅓ cup cider vinegar

1 tsp soy sauce

¼ cup julienned Harvest House Bell Pepper

1 (8 oz) can apricot halves, drained and coarsely chopped

- In saucepan, combine cornstarch, ginger and garlic.
- Gradually stir in broth, sorghum, vinegar and soy sauce.
- Over medium high heat, heat to boiling, stirring constantly; boil 1 minute.
- Stir in green pepper strips and apricots; heat thoroughly.
- Can be used with any stir-fried meat.
- Makes 2½ cups.

The LL&FG hired four hundred fifty workers, four hundred of them Chinese who earned twenty cents a day. The fifty Civil War veterans employed earned seventy-five cents a day, one dollar if they had a horse.

In the spring of 1867, the workers began cutting down trees to get the wood needed for ties and bridges. In June, the railroad ordered its locomotives, rails and tie plates from Liverpool, England. Because the American Civil War had ended just two years earlier, those materials were not readily available from U.S. manufacturers.

In September, the equipment, including a locomotive, arrived in Lawrence on the north side of the Kansas River. The workers spent two months building a temporary bridge to get the engine across to the south bank. That completed, they began laying track in earnest because of a rapidly approaching deadline that Lane faced.

The Douglas and Franklin county voters had seen and heard too many fly-by-night speculators to be taken in by another one. It didn't matter that the prestigious senator had given his word that the railroad would be completed on time. They wanted a guarantee. In order for the bonds to pay off, the voters stipulated, trains had to be running within a year.

The crews labored in two shifts, 'round the clock. Night work was made possible with the aid of the locomotive's brilliant headlight.

On December 30, only two miles of track remained to be laid. Track layers, or "gandy dancers," placed the rails on top of the frozen ground and, although the locomotive weaved as it followed the temporary tracks, the Leavenworth, Lawrence and Fort Gibson Railroad met the imposed deadline. The rail sections were made permanent the next spring.

The railroad later went through several name changes, and a bankruptcy before being taken over by the Atchison, Topeka and Santa Fe railroad lines in 1880. That company pulled out in the 1970's and in the 1980's sold track rights near Baldwin City to the Midland and Santa Fe Trail historical societies. Trains rolled again in 1987, making it possible to reach "Nowhere"—but nowhere beyond.

Chinese Plum Sauce

2 (16 oz) cans plums in heavy syrup, drained; save syrup

¾ cup water

1 tbsp vegetable oil

¼ tsp each clove, ginger, anise seed, and pepper

¾ tsp cinnamon

½ tsp each cumin, dry mustard

½ cup canned tomato sauce

1 medium Pickett's Gardens Onion, chopped

1 tbsp each soy sauce and Worcestershire

¼ tsp hot pepper sauce

1 tbsp wine vinegar

- Remove pits from plums
- Blend plums with 1¼ cups of the syrup and water until puréed; set aside.
- Discard remaining syrup.
- Heat oil in a 4 qt pan on medium high heat; stir spices into hot oil.
- Add plum purée, tomato sauce, onion, soy, Worcestershire and pepper seasoning.
- Boil uncovered, stirring often, until reduced to 3 cups, about 25 minutes.
- Stir in vinegar; serve warm.
- Keeps 3 weeks.
- Makes 3 cups.

Explorer Zebulon Montgomery Pike stopped in a Pawnee Indian Village while passing through Kansas in 1806. He was on his way to Colorado, a trip that would result in one of that state's highest peaks being named after him.

As Pike held council with the Pawnee he spotted a Spanish flag, left shortly before by an expedition from Mexico, flying in the village. A persuasive man, he convinced the Indians to replace it with the American flag, the first known to permanently fly in Kansas.

Within twenty years of Pike's visit the Pawnee had left the area. Dust became dirt and covered the village, preserving it for present-day archaeologists.

Three miles southwest of Republic, Kansas, a modern museum is constructed around the floor of one of the Pawnee earthlodges. Artifacts excavated at the valuable "dig" are also displayed at this unique museum operated by the Kansas State Historical Society.

Pikes Peak in Kansas? It used to be. Until 1861, the Kansas Territory included a sizable portion of present day Colorado.

Even some Nebraskans wanted to join us. One of the delegates representing them at the Kansas constitutional convention meeting at Wyandotte (present Kansas City) in 1859, said that the "Platte River is the natural northern boundary of Kansas while our present boundary is only an imaginary one." The resolution was defeated by ten votes. If it had been approved, Nebraska would have had to come up with another state capital. Lincoln would have been in northeast Kansas.

The Kansas Territory had several capitals before it was decided Topeka should be the permanent home for a state house. First

MAIN DISHES

Honey Creek Schoolhouse, Beloit

governor Andrew Reeder established a temporary seat of government at Fort Leavenworth in 1854. The first legislature met at Pawnee, on the Fort Riley military reservation, in 1855. After five days, it adjourned to the Shawnee Methodist Mission near Kansas City. That same year a bogus legislature meeting in a two-story frame building in the town of Lecompton, fourteen miles east of Topeka, drafted a constitution. The pro-slavery document was supported by President James Buchanan and Congress went so far as to appropriate $50,000 for a capitol building. It was never completed. Kansas entered the Union as a Free State in 1861. Lecompton Constitution Hall is now a national landmark.

Topeka has prospered as the seat of Kansas government. It became a railroad town when Cyrus K. Holliday started building the Atchison, Topeka & Santa Fe from there. It also has become a regional retail center, the headquarters city of numerous state associations, a major industrial and distribution center for the state, and home to Washburn University.

Attractions and events abound in the capital city. The Topeka Civic Theatre has won national awards for its productions. Washburn's "Ichabod" men's basketball team was a recent national small college champion. Heartland Park raceway is a world class motor sports complex. The Kansas Expocentre's offerings include such popular shows as Ringling Brothers, Barnum & Bailey Circus, ice spectaculars and concerts by top performers.

Among Topeka's most visited attractions is the five-story state capitol building. Inside are murals by native-born artist John Steuart Curry. His famous *Tragic Prelude* depicts enraged abolitionist John Brown, a rifle in his right hand and a bible in his left, surrounded by pro- and anti-slavery forces. It is symbolic of the turbulent territorial era when Kansas was known throughout the world as "Bleeding Kansas."

Curry never finished all of the other murals he planned for the building. Criticisms of his work prompted him to call a halt to his project. As a sidenote, Lumen Winter and his son finished the murals a few years ago.

Spanish Rice Casserole
"Celebrate! Kansas Food" Contest Winner

½ lb ground beef

3 tbsp Steffen's Butter

1 cup chopped Meier's Market Onions

½ cup chopped Meier's Market Green Pepper

⅓ cup chopped celery

2 Meier's Market Tomatoes, chopped

¼ tsp Carey Salt

2 cups cooked rice

½ lb Alma Colby Cheese, grated

- Brown ground beef; drain.
- In large skillet, sauté onion, green pepper and celery in butter.
- Add ground beef, tomatoes and salt; simmer 5 minutes.
- Layer rice and tomato mixture in 9" x 9" x 2" baking dish.
- Bake in 350 degree oven for 40 minutes.
- Top with grated cheese; return to oven until cheese is melted.
- Serves 4-6.

Festive Chicken with Asparagus

3 chicken breasts, halved

2 tbsp W-R All-Purpose Flour

3 tbsp vegetable oil

¼ cup crumbled bleu cheese

¼ cup Balkan Winery Dry White Wine

1 (10.75 oz) can cream of chicken soup

1 lb Pendleton's Fresh Asparagus

- Coat chicken with flour; brown in oil.
- In shallow, 3 qt casserole, mix bleu cheese, wine and soup.
- Arrange chicken in soup; spoon some over chicken to coat.
- Bake, uncovered, at 375 degrees for 30 minutes.
- Clean asparagus spears; cut in half, crosswise.
- Remove chicken from oven and arrange asparagus between chicken.
- Cover tightly and bake 30 minutes, or until chicken is tender.
- Serves 6.

Remember the Ovaltine mugs that featured Little Orphan Annie? How about Veg-O-Matics? Or gravity-feed gasoline pumps? Did you watch "Gunsmoke" every Saturday night?

Even if your answer is "no" I guarantee you'll be fascinated by the items and events displayed in the "Our Recent Past" exhibit at the Kansas Museum of History, west of Topeka. One highlight, the 1950's Rainbow Diner, doesn't serve anything but good information. After sitting down at the counter, Dorothy the waitress on a video screen, takes your orders and explains the food's nutritional value. Then Eldon, a long-time diner customer, chats with you about the history of Kansas agriculture.

Next to the diner the many fast foods that have been created in Kansas, and the franchises that have come to the state, are exhibited under an early McDonald's golden arch, taken from the first such restaurant in Topeka.

A small theater within the "Our Recent Past" gallery features a video film exploring the many world, national and state events and movements that had an impact on the lives of Kansans from 1940 to 1980. You'll relive each decade through newsreel shots, mixed with Kansas photos and home movies. Popular music of the time adds a nostalgic touch to the presentation.

"I Think I Will Like Kansas," is the exhibit which covers the years following the Civil War when central and western Kansas were settled. During this period, settlers from Europe and the eastern United States transformed the state into a patchwork quilt of farms, ranches and towns.

Featured in the display is the antique Santa Fe steam locomotive, the *Cyrus K. Holliday,* as well as a 1911 Santa Fe business car, and a 1920 drovers' car.

Gage Park, near the museum, is a popular place to picnic, swim, jog, or take the kids to play. Everyone enjoys riding the antique carousel and the miniature train which runs throughout the park.

The World Famous Topeka Zoo boasts a Tropical Rain Forest. Birds fly free under the huge, transparent dome, while iguanas lounge in the lush

Grandma's Chicken & Noodles

1 (1-3 lb) stewing hen
8 cups water
1 (14 oz) bag Helmuth's Homemade Noodles
1 tbsp dried onion
3 oz processed cheese spread

- Place hen in large stock pot and cover with water; cook until tender.
- Remove hen; debone and set meat aside.
- Bring chicken broth to boil; add noodles. Cook noodles 6-8 minutes, until tender.
- Add meat and cheese spread to noodles; bring to boil to reheat.
- Serves 8.

Chicken Enchiladas

1 chicken, cooked and deboned
1 (10.5 oz) can cream of chicken soup
1 (4 oz) can green chilies
1 (8 oz) ctn sour cream
12-14 El Toro Flour Tortillas
½ lb Alma Cheddar Cheese, shredded
¼ lb Alma Pepper Jack Cheese, shredded
sliced black olives

- In mixing bowl, combine chicken, soup, chilies and sour cream.
- Mix thoroughly; spoon filling onto each tortilla.
- Roll up and place seam side down in 9" x 13" baking pan.
- Cover with cheeses. Garnish with black olives.
- Bake in 350 degree oven for 45 minutes.
- Serves 8-10.

tropical vegetation. You'll enjoy looking for the "hidden critters" that blend into the jungle surroundings.

At the Discovering Apes Building you can view orangutans either from a tree house or from a glass tunnel, and get nose-to-nose with four hundred-pound gorillas cavorting in a natural setting.

The Lion's Pride exhibit, simulating southern and eastern Africa, has received rave reviews for its three virtually unobstructed and unique views of the big cats . . . one from the trail leading into the exhibit, one through thick glass in a cavern at the kopje rock outcropping, and the last through the various holes in the blind at the bush camp. The lions' waterhole is positioned directly in front of the glass window in the cavern so their drinking behaviors can be easily studied.

Want to see Dolly Parton, Jiminy Cricket and Mr. Lincoln? Look for them in Gage Park's internationally famous Reinisch Rose Garden. They're some of the uniquely named flowers among the hundreds of varieties that bloom from June through October.

Directly outside the main garden, along the east fence, lies the Parent-Progeny garden which exhibits genetically related rose groups. Traits inherited from the "parent" roses can be viewed in the "children" or "progeny" roses.

Also on the east side is the J. Glenn Logan Test Garden. It is one of only twenty-three official All-America Rose Selection (AARS) Test Gardens in the entire country. Here, newly hybridized roses, identified only by number, are grown and evaluated over a two-year period.

West of the main garden is a display garden containing a collection of all the AARS winners.

Topeka's historical Ward-Meade home was built in 1870 and is open to the public. The largest peacock fountain in the world is located in the surrounding five-acre park.

Combat Air Museum at Forbes Field has a good collection of vintage

Chicken Burritos

2 lbs chicken, cooked and diced

1 (16 oz) jar The Whole Enchilada's Mexican Salsa

1 (1.25 oz) pkg Williams Taco Seasoning

1 tbsp diced onion (optional)

¼ cup cornstarch

¼ cup cold water

8 La Siesta Flour Tortillas, heated

Suggested Toppings:

grated cheese

shredded lettuce

sliced black olives

diced tomatoes

sour cream

- Combine chicken, salsa, taco seasoning and onion in saucepan.
- Mix cornstarch and cold water together; add to chicken mixture.
- Cover and simmer 10 minutes.
- Spread ½ cup chicken mixture in center of each tortilla.
- Add desired toppings and fold in both sides of tortilla toward center.
- Serves 8.

Build-Your-Own Burritos

2 cups cooked pork or beef roast, diced or shredded

2 cups cooked pinto beans with liquid

¼ cup chopped onion (optional)

1 tbsp Ken's Blend Chili Seasoning

8 La Siesta Flour Tortillas

Suggested Toppings:

shredded lettuce

chopped tomato

grated Longhorn cheese

Pedro Lopez Taco Sauce

- Combine meat, beans, onion and chili seasoning.
- Cook 15-20 minutes.
- Place meat mixture on a warm tortilla and top with lettuce, tomato, cheese and taco sauce.
- Roll to enclose filling.
- Serves 4.

military aircraft. The museum's popular annual fund raiser, "Superbatics," attracts thousands of spectators to see performances by top precision flying acts, vintage aircraft, and the latest jet planes.

Railroad Days, over Labor Day weekend, celebrates Topeka's railroad heritage with big trains, model trains and railroad memorabilia. A special passenger excursion train operates in conjunction with the event. If you want to ride, get your reservations in early.

The Topeka area has two truly unique bed and breakfast inns. One is the Heritage House, the other is The Barn.

Heritage House is the site where Drs. C.F., Karl and Will Menninger established their world famous mental health clinic in 1925. It is listed on the National Register of Historic Places.

The three-story, white frame house has a native stone front porch and fifteen guest bedrooms, all with private baths. Dr. Karl's Study, and Dr. Will's Study, are guest rooms containing mementos and reminders of both men.

Dining at Heritage House is an experience similar to those one would have at intimate, cosmopolitan restaurants in cities like Chicago and Boston. The pace is unhurried ... my last meal there lasted more than three hours ... because everything is done to perfection.

My wife, Pat, had the Hawaiian Ono with macadamia nuts, a delicate fish. My beef entree was Entrecote Au Poivre Flambé. Our appetizer was crab bourbon bisque and dessert was a triple chocolate torte.

A word of caution. Heritage House isn't for those who are pinching pennies.

The Barn was built just thirty years after President James Buchanan signed the bill making Kansas the thirty-fourth state. It is operated by Tom Ryan, his wife, Marcella and their daughter, Patricia. Until a few years back, the bed and breakfast inn housed their pigs and other livestock.

Tortilla Chip Casserole

1½ lbs ground pork, beef or lamb

1 medium onion, finely chopped

2 (8 oz) cans tomato sauce

1 (4 oz) can diced green chilies

2 tsp leaf oregano

½ tsp salt

1 (8 oz) pkg Spanish Gardens Tortilla Chips

½ lb Alma Monterey Jack Cheese, cut in ½" cubes

1 cup sour cream, room temperature

⅓ cup grated Alma Cheddar Cheese

- In skillet, cook ground meat and onion until meat is brown and onion is tender; drain fat.
- Add tomato sauce, chilies, oregano and salt.
- Simmer sauce, uncovered, for 10 minutes; remove from heat.
- Layer in 2 qt casserole, in order, half the tortilla chips, Monterey Jack cheese and meat sauce. Repeat.
- Bake 20 minutes in 325 degree oven.
- Remove from oven and spread sour cream on top; sprinkle with Cheddar cheese; broil until cheese melts.
- Serve immediately.
- Serves 6-8.

Mediterranean Pasta

1 lb Das Smokehaus Smoked Sausage

2 medium onions, thinly sliced

1 small clove garlic, minced

1 tbsp olive oil

2 medium Harvest House Zucchini, thinly sliced

½ tsp dried basil

¼ tsp dried oregano

¼ tsp salt

dash black pepper

2 large tomatoes, seeded and cut into large pieces

hot cooked Pasta Mills Spaghetti

grated Parmesan cheese (optional)

- Break sausage into pieces and cook in large skillet until lightly browned; drain and set aside.
- Place onions, garlic and oil in same skillet.
- Sauté and stir over medium heat until onions are soft and lightly browned.
- Add zucchini, basil, oregano, salt and pepper; cook 5 minutes.
- Add tomatoes; cover and simmer 10 minutes, stirring occasionally.
- Serve over spaghetti with Parmesan cheese.
- Serves 4-5.

"We were barely making ends meet," recalls Tom. "I had always dreamed of being in the hospitality business, and owning an inn, so we finally made our break. We gutted the barn, made it into a comfortable inn, and moved there ourselves."

The Ryans were apprehensive as to how The Barn would be accepted. They needn't have been. Recently the inn had to be expanded to eighteen rooms to accommodate business. In the process, an indoor swimming pool was added.

The rooms are well appointed, with king-size beds and private baths. Breakfasts are good down home country cookin' and often include bacon, eggs, pancakes, cereals, fruits, and more. The Ryans don't stop cooking until you stop eating.

An evening meal, upon arrival, is included in The Barn's overnight package. Ham, beef, whatever suits the Ryan's fancy. It's difficult to understand how, with all the delicious food before them every night, they stay so slender.

Gerat H. Hollenberg was a German immigrant who, after trying his luck for three years in the gold fields of California and then in Australian and Peruvian mines, was traveling west on the Oregon Trail. When he reached the high bluffs two miles northeast of the present community of Hanover, he established a trading station and prospered by providing supplies to the many wagon trains that passed.

Hollenberg's station served as a family home, a neighborhood store and a tavern. In 1860 mail began arriving there once a week, from both the east and west, via the fastest and most dangerous postal service of the time, the Pony Express. From June 1 until July 1, 1861, service was expanded to twice a week. On October 25, 1861, it ceased.

That wasn't the end of the station's importance to the westward movement, however. The Holliday Stage Line used it for a stop on its Atchison-Sacramento route for changing teams of horses.

Santa Fe Chorizo Pie
Winning Recipe from 1990 Kansas Egg Recipe Contest

Crust:
1 cup all-purpose flour

½ tsp salt

½ tsp dried parsley flakes

¾ tsp dried basil

¼ tsp cumin

6 tbsp vegetable shortening

3 tbsp cold water

1 egg white

Filling:
½ lb Terry's Smoky Hill Chorizo Sausage, casing removed

4 eggs

1¾ cups milk

⅓ cup chopped orange, red or green bell pepper

2 tbsp chopped green chilies

1 tbsp snipped fresh chives

2 hard cooked eggs, chopped

1 cup shredded Monterey Jack cheese

- Combine flour, salt, parsley flakes, basil and cumin. Cut in shortening.
- Sprinkle in water, 1 tbsp at a time. mixing until flour is moistened and dough almost cleans sides of bowl.
- Form dough into a ball and place on a lightly floured surface.
- Roll into 11″ circle; ease into a 9″ pie plate. Trim edge and flute.
- Chill while preparing filling, about 20 minutes.
- Crumble chorizo into 9″ skillet; brown and drain. Set aside.
- Beat 4 eggs with milk. Add bell pepper, chilies, chives and chopped eggs; mix well.
- Prick bottom and sides of crust with fork. Line with foil and bake 5 minutes.
- Remove foil, brush with egg white; return to oven another 5 minutes.
- Remove from oven. Sprinkle chorizo and cheese on bottom of crust. Pour egg mixture on top of meat and cheese.
- Bake at 375 degrees, 40 minutes, until knife inserted halfway into center comes out clean.
- Let stand 5 minutes before cutting.
- Serves 6.

The Hollenberg Station remains as the only unaltered Pony Express stop, in its original location. It is a long, frame structure with six rooms on the ground floor. In one of them, Hollenberg kept a small stock of groceries and dry goods and operated an unofficial post office. Another room served as a bar and tavern. The rest were used for family living. Upstairs a loft ran the length of the building and here stagecoach and Pony Express employees had a common sleeping room.

Nearby is a large stable capable of housing one hundred horses and oxen. Fresh mounts for Pony Express riders were kept there.

The property is a registered National Historic Landmark and is open to the public.

Pony Express Station No. 1, in nearby Marysville, is also preserved as a museum. It was the first stop for riders heading west from St. Joseph, Missouri, where the service originated.

The bluestem pasture region of Kansas is one of the great grazing lands of the world. More commonly called the Flint Hills, the virtually treeless pastures comprise the last large segment of true prairie. Buffalo have been replaced by cattle. Nearly one million of them are shipped here each year to be fattened on the nutritious grasses.

There's no better time to see the Flint Hills than in the spring, after the ranchers have burned away the scrub brush, and the grass takes on an emerald hue. The "brush burns," themselves, are a spectacular sight. Controlled fires dot the horizon as far as the eye can see. At night, the flames light up the skies giving them an eerie glow.

Emporia, Manhattan, and Council Grove are some of the larger Flint Hills communities. William Allen White, Pulitzer Prize-winning editor and publisher of the Emporia Gazette, brought fame to his city. Emporia State University is also located there.

Manhattan is a major retail center for the region, and home to Kansas State University. The school is internationally recognized for its

Ham and Swiss Cheese Casserole A' La Spaghetti

"Celebrate! Kansas Food" Contest Winner

5 tbsp Steffen's Butter

1 (8 oz) can mushroom pieces, drained

2 cups cooked cubed OhSe Ham

5 cups Meyer's Garden Spot and Greenhouse Spaghetti Squash, cooked and drained

1 medium Meyer's Garden Spot and Greenhouse Onion, diced

3 tbsp Stafford County Flour Mills All-Purpose Flour

1 cup hot chicken broth

¾ cup Steffen's Milk, scalded

¾ cup grated Swiss cheese, divided

1½ tsp Dijon mustard

¼ tsp Carey Salt

⅛ tsp pepper

½ cup grated Parmesan cheese

½ cup slivered almonds

- In large skillet, melt butter.
- Sauté mushrooms and ham briefly; remove and place in bowl with squash.
- Sauté onion in butter remaining in skillet; blend in flour and gradually add chicken broth and milk, stirring until thick and smooth.
- Add ½ cup Swiss cheese, mustard, salt and pepper; stir until cheese is melted.
- Combine with squash mixture.
- Place in buttered 9″ x 12″ baking dish; cover and bake in 350 degree oven for 20-30 minutes.
- Remove from oven; sprinkle with Parmesan, remaining Swiss cheese and almonds.
- Place under broiler until bubbly.
- Serves 6.

Polish Sausage and Cabbage Casserole

1 small head cabbage, shredded

1 pkg Das Smokehaus Polish Sausage

¾ cup water

salt and pepper to taste

- Place shredded cabbage in skillet with sausage on top.
- Cover with water and sprinkle with salt and pepper.
- Cover and bring to a boil; simmer for 45 minutes.
- Slice sausages before serving.
- Serves 4-6.

contributions to agriculture, particularly in the field of grain science.

Konza Prairie Research Natural Area, used by Kansas State for ecological research and education, contains over eight thousand six hundred acres of tallgrass prairie. Much of it can be seen from Interstate Highway 70.

The American Institute of Baking, another Manhattan research and teaching facility, is famous, across the globe, in the baking industry. It attracts many foreign students to its classes.

To the north of Manhattan is Tuttle Creek State Park & Reservoir. Approximately fifty miles long, the lake is ideal for boating and other water recreation.

Council Grove, south of Manhattan and one hundred two miles from Kansas City, is recognized as the birthplace of the Santa Fe Trail. Here, in a grove of trees that gave the community its name, a treaty was negotiated in 1825 with the Osage tribe, that guaranteed travelers safe passage across the Indians' land.

Twelve historic sites are included in a driving tour of Council Grove. Council Oak, the Old Kaw Mission and the Pioneer Jail are some of the stops. A cache at the base of Post Office Oak Tree served as a crude post office for pack trains and caravans from 1825 to 1847. Last Chance Store afforded a final opportunity, between points east and Santa Fe, to buy sowbelly, beans, whiskey and other supplies.

Council Grove's Hays House is the oldest restaurant west of the Mississippi River. It still dispenses good food. Many of its recipes, including those for Beulah's ham and grasshopper pie, have been publicized in nationally distributed culinary publications.

Many of us can remember Saturday afternoons spent cheering at our neighborhood theater as the U.S. Cavalry arrived on the big screen, just in the nick of time, to save a small band of settlers from attacking Indians.

Louisiana Red Sauce over Linguine

1 (12 oz) pkg linguine
2 (15 oz) cans tomato sauce
1 tbsp olive oil
1/3 cup Trader Bill's Special Blend
1 clove garlic, minced
1 tsp Worcestershire sauce
1/2 cup Fields of Fair White Wine (medium dry)
1 tbsp brown sugar
1-2 tsp Olde Westport Cajun Spice (optional)
1 lb Ernie's Hickory Smoked Sausage or Ham

- Cook linguine according to pkg directions; drain.
- Place all remaining ingredients, except meat, in saucepan and bring to boil over medium heat.
- Turn down heat and simmer for 15 minutes, stirring often.
- Prepare and cut up sausage or ham.
- Add meat to sauce, cook 5 minutes longer.
- Serve over linguine.
- Serves 6.

Wagon Wheel Skillet

1 (6 oz) pkg hash brown potato mix
1 cube chicken bouillon
1½ cups boiling water
3 tbsp Steffen's Butter
½ cup chopped onion
½ cup chopped green pepper
⅓ cup chopped celery
¼ cup fresh chopped parsley
1½ cups creamed large curd cottage cheese
¾ cup sour cream
⅛ tsp black pepper
1 lb OhSe Dinner Franks
2 slices American cheese
¼ cup sliced green onions

- Combine hash brown mix, bouillon and water in mixing bowl; mix well and let stand 10 minutes.
- Melt butter in 12″ skillet. Sauté onion, green pepper and celery 4 minutes, until tender.
- Stir potato mixture, parsley, cottage cheese, sour cream and pepper into skillet.
- Cut franks almost in half lengthwise, leaving 1 side attached.
- Cut cheese slices into 4 strips each; place 1 strip in each frank.
- Arrange franks on top of potatoes in "spoke" fashion.
- Cover skillet; heat 10 minutes or until thoroughly heated.
- Garnish with sliced green onions.
- Serves 4.

Hollywood would have had us believe that the life of a horse soldier was a glamorous one. Certainly there were exciting battles. But most days were uneventful, spent training or performing such routine tasks as cleaning out stables.

The U.S. Cavalry Museum at Fort Riley, near Junction City, introduces visitors to the role this elite group played in the opening of the west. Galleries illustrate the development of the military saddle, horse equipment and uniforms, and provide a look at the weapons used during the service's many periods of transition.

Fort Riley has been home to the U.S. Cavalry since the 1800's. The last horse-mounted units were phased out in the 1940's.

The famous Seventh Cavalry Regiment was organized at the fort in 1866. Through huge dioramas, slide presentations and exhibits, the museum tells its story, and that of Black Buffalo Soldiers; the Cavalry's role in such historical encounters as the battles at Cimarron Crossing and Downers Station, and the massacre at Wounded Knee; and of some of the distinguished officers . . . including J. E. B. Stuart and George S. Patton, Jr. . . . who once were stationed at the fort.

Complementing the exhibits is a fine art gallery featuring the works of many talented contemporary artists and two Frederic Remington originals.

"The proudest thing I can claim is that I am from Abilene . . ." Dwight D. Eisenhower told a hometown crowd honoring him after World War II. ". . . Through this world it has been my fortune or misfortune to wander at considerable distance. Never has this town been outside my heart and memory."

Abilene was proud of him, too. He was a five-star general, supreme commander of the allied nations' military forces, and planner of the successful D-Day invasion.

Few of the people "Ike" had grown up around expected greatness from

Sausage Squash Pecan Casserole
"Celebrate! Kansas Food" Contest Winner

2 lbs J. C. Meier & Sons Yellow Squash, sliced ½" thick
4 tbsp butter
2 medium onions, sliced
1 clove garlic, finely chopped
1 cup milk
1 cup Rainbo Bread Crumbs
1 lb Peabody Sausage House Sausage, cooked and crumbled
4 eggs, lightly beaten
1½ cups grated Alma Sharp Cheddar Cheese
1 cup chopped Carden Pecans
½ tsp Carey Salt
pepper

Topping:
4 tbsp melted butter
½ cup Rainbo Bread Crumbs
½ cup chopped Carden Pecans

- Grease a 2 qt casserole; set aside.
- Cook sliced squash in heavy pan, adding enough water to cover.
- Bring to a boil; reduce heat and simmer until the squash is soft enough to mash. Drain and mash.
- Melt butter in a separate pan; add the onions and garlic and sauté until soft. Add squash.
- Heat milk and stir in bread crumbs, sausage, eggs, cheese, pecans, salt and pepper; pour into buttered casserole.
- For topping, combine melted butter, bread crumbs and pecans.
- Sprinkle over casserole.
- Bake in 350 degree oven for 30 minutes.
- Serves 4-6.

Burger Bean Bake

2 slices bacon, cut in small pieces
1 medium onion, chopped
1 lb ground chuck
2 (1 lb) cans pork and beans
½ cup ketchup
½ cup Golden Mill Sorghum
½ tsp dry mustard
1 tbsp Worcestershire sauce

- Fry bacon and remove bits.
- Sauté onions in bacon drippings.
- Add ground chuck and brown.
- Combine all ingredients; pour into baking dish, and bake at 375 degrees for 30 minutes.
- Serves 12-16.

him. He was a nice fellow, all right, but he had a limited future working with his father in the Belle Springs Creamery. As a fireman and refrigeration helper he wasn't exactly going places. It wasn't until he was appointed to West Point, two years after graduating from high school, that his military career began.

More than twenty years of routine assignments later the name Eisenhower wasn't a household word. It soon would be. In 1942, Ike was named Commander-in-Chief of the Allied forces in North Africa. Within a year the Germans had been ousted from the continent, Sicily was conquered, and Italy was neutralized as an Axis power.

An impressed President Franklin Delano Roosevelt named Eisenhower to plan and direct the invasion of Europe. In 1944 it was launched. Eleven months later Germany signed an unconditional surrender.

After the war, Ike served as chief of staff of the United States Army, president of Columbia University, and Supreme Allied Commander of the North Atlantic Treaty Organization (NATO) in Europe. He was elected President of the United States in 1953 and won a second term in 1956.

As president, Ike signed legislation that continues to affect the lives of most Americans. He authorized the interstate highway system and the U.S. Commission on Civil Rights. His signature enabled Alaska and Hawaii to become states. And his commitment to American culture is chronicled in the National Cultural Center for the Performing Arts in Washington, D.C., which was later renamed the John F. Kennedy Center for the Performing Arts.

Kansas, and America, celebrates the life of Dwight David Eisenhower at the five-building Eisenhower Center in Abilene.

Ike's final resting place—and that of his wife, "Mamie," and their first-born son, Doud Dwight—is in a chapel entitled "A Place of Meditation." A motion picture, shown in the Visitor's Center auditorium, reviews the life and work of the famed statesman, politician and military leader.

Stir-Fried Asparagus and Pork

1 lb Knackstedt's Fresh Asparagus

1 small hot red pepper (optional)

2 tbsp vegetable oil

1 lb Lone Pine Farms Pork Tenderloin, cut in quarters lengthwise and then cut ¼" thick

1 clove garlic, finely chopped

6 green onions, cut in 1" pieces, including tops

1 tbsp Chinese oyster sauce

1 tbsp soy sauce

1 tbsp dry sherry

- Slice asparagus diagonally into 1½" pieces, keeping tips whole.
- If using hot pepper, cut into thin slivers, removing seeds.
- Heat oil in a wok or large skillet until sizzling hot. Stir-fry pork for 3-4 minutes, until no pink remains.
- Remove with slotted spoon; set aside.
- Add garlic and asparagus to pan stir-fry several minutes until crisp tender.
- Return pork to pan along with green onions, oyster sauce, soy sauce and sherry. Cook until pork is heated thoroughly.
- Serve immediately.
- Serves 4-6.

Incredible Rice Frittata

½ cup finely chopped onion

1 tbsp butter

8 Sunnyfresh Farms Eggs

½ cup milk

½ tsp salt

1 tsp Worcestershire sauce

¼ tsp hot pepper sauce

2 cups cooked rice

1 (4 oz) can chopped green chilies, undrained

1 medium Meier's Market Tomato, chopped

½ cup shredded Pioneer Cheddar Cheese

- In 10" skillet, sauté onion in butter until tender.
- Blend eggs, milk and seasonings.
- Stir in rice, chilies and tomato. Pour into pan.
- Cover and cook over medium low heat until eggs are almost set, 12-15 minutes.
- Sprinkle with cheese.
- Remove from heat; let stand, covered, about 10 minutes.
- Serves 4.

Scenic trails, Winfield

Pork and Corn Casserole

Filling:

1 lb Lone Pine Farms Ground Pork

½ tsp salt

½ tsp Pedro Lopez Chili Powder

1 cup shredded Pioneer Cheddar Cheese

½ cup Hayward's Pit Bar-B-Que Sauce

1½ cans Mexicorn whole kernel corn, drained

1 (8 oz) can tomato sauce

Crust:

1 cup HearTland Mill® Whole Wheat Flour

½ cup HearTland Mill® Yellow Corn Meal

2 tbsp sugar

1 tsp salt

1 tsp baking powder

¼ cup butter

½ cup milk

1 egg, beaten

1 cup shredded Pioneer Cheddar Cheese, divided

- Brown pork; stir in remaining filling ingredients and set aside.
- Stir together flour, corn meal, sugar, salt and baking powder and cut in butter.
- Blend in milk, egg and half the cheese.
- Spread crust mixture over bottom and sides of a greased 9″ baking pan.
- Pour filling into crust; bake in 400 degree oven for 25-30 minutes.
- Sprinkle with remaining cheese during last few minutes of baking.
- Serves 6-8.

Catfish and Rice

4 tbsp butter

2 cups cooked, flaked Culver Fish Farm Catfish

1 cup cooked rice

2 Sunnyfresh Farms Eggs, hard cooked and separated

salt and pepper

- Melt butter in iron skillet. Add fish, rice and finely chopped egg whites.
- Salt and pepper to taste.
- Stir gently and heat thoroughly.
- Serve on hot platter; garnish with grated egg yolks.
- Serves 4.

Eisenhower's boyhood home, a simple white frame house on Fourth Street ("I don't know yet how my mother jammed us all in," he wrote), remains in the exact location where the president and his five brothers grew to manhood. Visitors can view original furnishings and fixtures used by the family.

In the lobby of the museum are murals depicting Ike's life and career from his early childhood through his service as president. Exhibits in five major galleries contain items associated with him and the members of his family. These range from gifts that heads of state from around the world bestowed on him, to the simple artifacts of everyday life.

Eisenhower was an accomplished amateur artist whose interest in painting stemmed from his wife's portrait being painted in 1948. When the professional artist took a break, Ike picked up a brush and started dabbling on some scrap canvas. From that point, until his death in 1969, he used painting as a form of relaxation and self-expression.

Among Ike's favorite types of paintings were portraits and landscapes. His renderings of Abraham Lincoln and George Washington, along with a number of landscapes, are exhibited at the Eisenhower Center.

Across the highway from the Eisenhower complex "Dutchess" reigns over a unique museum dedicated to dogs. A greyhound, the former sprinter is more the queen of The Greyhound Hall of Fame. From her perch, just inside the entrance, she surveys her domain. Those who approach usually can pet her but, if she's not in the mood for courtiers, she may abruptly leave.

The museum traces the history of the greyhound species back to 5,000 B.C. A movie and a miniature race track, among other exhibits, provide insight on the fast-paced sport.

Old Abilene Town and Western Museum, and The Museum of Independent Telephony and Dickinson County Historical Museum, are other attractions near the Eisenhower Center. I love to ride the handcarved carousel at the county museum. It was built in Abilene at the turn of the century.

Gourmet Cheese Casserole

½ lb wide egg noodles

1 tbsp vegetable oil

1 lb ground beef

1 (6 oz) can tomato paste

1½ cups water

1 clove garlic, minced

2 tsp salt

¾ tsp oregano leaves

¼ tsp pepper

1 (4 oz) pkg cream cheese, softened

⅓ (3 oz) cup Steffen's Sour Cream

⅔ cup cottage cheese

1 (4 oz) pkg Alma Mozzarella Cheese, shredded and divided

⅓ cup chopped onion

2 tbsp chopped green pepper

1 tsp crushed basil

½ tsp garlic powder

- Cook noodles according to pkg directions; drain.
- Cool by rinsing with cold water; drain. Toss with oil to prevent sticking.
- Brown ground beef; drain.
- Add tomato paste, water, garlic, salt, oregano and pepper. Cover; simmer 30 minutes, stirring occasionally.
- Remove from heat.
- Blend cream cheese and sour cream until smooth and creamy.
- On low speed, gradually add cottage cheese, ¼ cup mozzarella cheese, onion, green pepper, basil and garlic powder.
- Continue mixing until thoroughly blended.
- Grease 8" square pan.
- Layer half of meat sauce, noodles and cheese mixture. Repeat with noodles and cheese.
- Top with remaining meat sauce.
- Sprinkle with remaining mozzarella cheese; bake in 350 degree oven for 1 hour.
- Let stand 15-20 minutes before cutting.
- Serves 4.

Kirby House, in the downtown area, is one of three historic mansions open to the public. Guided tours are offered at the circa 1880's Lebold-Vasholtz home and the 1905 Georgian-style residence that was built by Dr. and Mrs. A.B. Seelye. Kirby House is recognized as Abilene's finest restaurant. Reservations are recommended.

I love a good ol' fashioned hamburger. Not the kind a popular national franchise touts, although they'll do, but those that were staples at neighborhood diners. Buns warmed atop grilling beef, lots of fried onions, and a long-time cook who didn't need a buzzer or a light to tell him when to flip the patties.

Salina still has one of those places. The Cozy Inn is a local legend that's even gained fame in New York. Nationally syndicated food columnists Jane and Michael Stern have described "cozies" as America's perfect lunch counter hamburgers.

Legions of cozy fanciers share their enthusiasm for the tasty little sandwiches. They sometimes go to extremes to satisfy their cravings for the three-bite size burger.

Bob Spreier, Cozy Inn night manager, recalls a former Salinan who showed up, when he was working the morning shift, and ordered six cozies.

"She was driving from Florida to California and saw a sign in Oklahoma City that said 'Salina, Kansas, and Points North.' It brought back memories of having come to the Cozy Inn, as a child, with her mom and dad."

"While she was eating," he continues, "I looked out the window and saw a guy, inside her car, who didn't look very happy. It was her husband. He had just woken up and didn't have any idea where they were.

"When she went outside and told him how far off course they were, he sure raised some cane! Finally, he calmed down and they both came

126

Reuben Strata

1 (14 oz) can sauerkraut

5 cups day-old cubed Home Town Cafe
Dark Rye Bread

6 oz Hiawatha Corned Beef, chopped

1½ cups shredded Swiss cheese, divided

½ cup chopped red onion

10 Sunnyfresh Farms Eggs

2 cups milk

½ cup thousand island dressing

2 tsp caraway seed

¼ tsp salt

¼ cup chopped green onion tops

- Drain sauerkraut; pressing spoon against sides of strainer to remove all liquid.
- Combine bread cubes, corned beef, 1 cup cheese and onion to drained sauerkraut; toss.
- Place mixture in a well-buttered 9" x 13" baking dish.
- Blend eggs, milk, dressing, caraway seed and salt. Pour over bread mixture.
- Cover and refrigerate several hours or overnight.
- Bake 45-55 minutes in 350 degree oven.
- Sprinkle with remaining cheese and green onion tops.
- Serves 8.

Quiche Lorraine in a Noodle Shell
Kansas Egg Recipe Contest, Winner
National Egg Recipe Contest, Second Prize

1 tbsp butter

6 oz thin noodles

4 eggs

1½ cups milk

1 cup shredded Swiss cheese

½ cup grated Parmesan cheese

½ cup chopped onion

1 (8 oz) pkg Hickory Point Bacon,
cooked and crumbled

¼ tsp salt

¼ tsp pepper

¼ tsp sweet basil

⅛ tsp nutmeg

- Butter a 10" pie plate.
- Prepare noodles according to pkg directions; drain.
- Line buttered pie plate with warm noodles.
- Beat eggs and milk; stir in cheeses, onion, bacon, salt, pepper, basil and nutmeg.
- Pour egg mixture into noodle crust.
- Bake in 375 degree oven for 30 minutes, or until center is set.
- Serves 8.

inside. After he ate a couple of cozies he was hooked. They ordered several dozen more to eat on the road."

Fried onions give cozies their distinctive odor which, according to the Cozy Inn's business manager, Dick Pickering, is a key to their nearly seventy-year success.

"If you come into the Cozy Inn for five minutes, and go anywhere else in town, people know where you've been," he says. "A cozy's smell is our best advertisement."

Pickering's wife, Kathryn, who owns the Cozy, chuckles in agreement.

"During World War II, Camp Phillips was located near here," she remembers. "The boys coming back from overseas came up with their own directions on how to get to the Cozy Inn.

"After you get off the bus by the Lamer Hotel," they instructed, "walk down to the bank corner. Turn right and continue to the Seventh Street corner. Then just follow your nose!"

The Cozy Inn was one of the earliest exponents of the fast food concept now so commonplace. Bob Kinkel purchased the six-stool eatery in 1922, three months after it opened. He operated it until his death in 1960. Kathryn, his widow, has run it ever since.

A cozy weighs a little more than an ounce before its four and one-half minute grilling, and is served on a three and one-half inch bun baked especially for it. Only bull meat, ninety-percent lean, is used.

Onions, fried with the hamburgers, are the real thing, not the instant kind many other restaurants serve.

All cozies are garnished with pickle slices. Customers have a choice of adding mustard and ketchup.

"We don't serve cheeseburgers and have never offered french fries," Kathryn says. Pop still comes in bottles. Chips are on a wall rack.

Other fast food chains haven't hurt the Cozy Inn's business.

"Sometimes their employees will come in here, in uniform, to get cozies," Kathryn says. "On occasion we even serve their bosses."

Television news correspondent Charles Kuralt finds much of the

Beef Fajitas

3 lbs Western Brand Meats Beef Skirts
or Flank Steaks, trimmed

1 tsp garlic powder

1 tsp cumin

½ tsp salt

½ tsp pepper

1 (16 oz) btl lite Italian dressing (not
creamy Italian)

12 La Siesta Flour Tortillas, warmed

1 (8 oz) jar Fuego Picante Sauce

2 cups grated cheese

½ cup chopped onion

2 cups shredded lettuce

1 cup sour cream

1 cup guacamole

- Cut meat across grain in strips
  1"-1½" wide by 5" long.
- Generously sprinkle all meat strips
  with garlic powder, cumin, salt and
  pepper.
- Place meat strips in a plastic
  container with a tight fitting lid;
  cover with the Italian dressing,
  thoroughly coating all pieces.
- Cover container and refrigerate for a
  minimum of 12 hours.
- Turn meat over in dressing 2 times
  during marination period.
- Prepare coals to medium hot
  temperature.
- Remove meat strips from dressing;
  drain and place on grill.
- Cover grill and cook 10-12 minutes,
  turning 3 times during cooking.
- Serve with flour tortillas, picante
  sauce, cheese, onion, lettuce, sour
  cream and guacamole.
- Serves 6.

material he uses for his *On The Road* series off the beaten path, in small towns and away from interstate highways. Northeast Kansas has many attractions—some natural, others made by human hands—that fit his criteria for unique, eccentric, or just darn interesting.

C oncordia, fifty miles north of Salina, is the Cloud County seat. During World War II, a camp nearby housed a large contingent of German prisoners of war. Some traces of it still exist. The city also is home to The Brown Grand Opera House, a magnificent 1906 structure completely restored with the original woodwork, interior design and Victorian furniture. It is listed on the National Register of Historic Places.

Concordia hosts the North Central Kansas Rodeo each August and is a favorite destination for canoeists who paddle the Republican River Canoe Trail.

Belleville, Concordia's neighbor to the north, is a mecca for auto-racing fans. Its high banks track of clay gumbo is considered the fastest half-mile dirt track in the world. The facility hosts the Miller Midget National Races each year and Indianapolis 500 winners, A.J. Foyt and Bobby Parsons, have raced there.

W ork crews on the Sinclair Oil Company's famous "oil highway," from Teapot Dome, Wyoming, to Freeman, Missouri, reached Cummings' farm, near Morrowville, in 1923. As construction crews laboriously backfilled his land by mules and slip scrapers, Cummings concluded that there had to be a better way. The teams couldn't begin to keep up with the trenching machinery used by the workmen.

After explaining his idea for a bulldozer to company officials, Cummings was encouraged to build a motorized prototype. But he also was given a short deadline.

MEATS & FISH

The Serene beauty of Kansas

"Jim told me Friday noon that something had to be built by 8 o'clock Monday morning," J. Earl McLeod, also of Morrowville, recalled in 1982. "I spent four hours at the drafting board, and we began gathering up odds and ends from junk yards all over Washington County. By Monday we were ready."

A main component of the bulldozer was a Model T frame. Other gadgetry included windmill springs and an assortment of automobile and tractor parts. McLeod said, "The bulldozer was crudely constructed but solidly built to stand the gaff. It was not overly pretty but it was hell for stout."

The 1925 patent copy for the machine was issued to both men. Their success prompted an order for five more tractor-powered bulldozers. The rest, as has often been said, is history.

A replica of the Cummings-McLeod machine is in Morrowville's Cummings Park.

Walt Kelley, the originator of the comic strip "Pogo," once referred to the sandstone formations at Rock City as "Jayhawk eggs."

"Taint laying 'em that's a chore, but land, hatchin' 'em shore do wear a body down!'" he said in a 1954 cartoon.

The natural geological wonder is located two and one-half miles southwest of the city of Minneapolis. The two hundred rocks are noted for their large size and varied shapes. Some are twenty-seven feet in diameter and are perfect spheres.

Legend has it that any young marriageable female able to crawl through the small hole in doughnut rock's center will not remain single long.

According to geologists the rocks are concretions, sand grains cemented together naturally at scattered points. Through the years they have resisted the elements' erosive activity to become a unique natural attraction, one of a kind on the planet.

Marinated Char-Broiled Beef

½ cup soy sauce

3 tbsp Sweetheart Honey

¼ cup cider vinegar

1 tbsp garlic powder

1 tbsp ginger

1½ cups vegetable oil

2 green onions, finely chopped

1 Hoseney's Beef Round Steak, 2" thick

- Blend first 7 ingredients for marinade.
- Pour marinade on steak; cover and marinate 4 hours. Turn steak once each hour.
- Drain off marinade and grill steak on outdoor grill for 15 minutes on each side (less time for very rare).
- Remove from grill; let stand 10 minutes before carving.
- Slice diagonally across the grain, as thin as possible.
- Serves 8-10.

Swiss Steak

2½ lbs Stoffle Meat Co. Round Steak, well trimmed

2 tbsp vegetable oil

3½ cups water

1 (3.25 oz) pkg Olde Westport Beef Sauce Mix

2 (14.5 oz) cans stewed tomatoes

1 medium onion, chopped

2 stalks celery, chopped

¼ tsp black pepper

- Cut meat into serving size pieces.
- Heat oil in large skillet; brown meat; remove.
- Add water to same skillet; stir in sauce mix and, stirring continuously, bring to boil over medium heat.
- When thickened, add tomatoes, onion, celery and pepper; stir.
- Bring to boil and simmer 5 minutes.
- Place meat in greased baking dish.
- Pour sauce mixture on top.
- Cover dish with foil. Bake in 350 degree oven for 1½ hours.
- Serves 4-6.

John M. Davis always was a loner, but particularly after his wife died. He never liked the folks in Hiawatha and they didn't much care for him.

The childless Davis' had accumulated a considerable amount of money over the years and the widower worried about what would become of it after he was gone. He came up with an elaborate plan to make sure no one would get his fortune.

Davis talked to the local monument salesman and ordered a tomb be built unlike any around. Eleven life-sized Italian marble statues would surround it, showing him and his wife at various stages in their lives, from courtship until he was left alone.

The eccentric and bizarre Davis Memorial is in Hiawatha's Mount Hope Cemetery, maintained by the local residents he disliked. Ironically, Davis spent so much money on the monument that he went broke and lived several years of his life in the county home.

SOUTHEAST KANSAS

The Osage Plains of Southeast Kansas give way to the Cherokee Lowland, in a region known as the "Little Balkans." The Osage Indians once prospered here as fur traders. The Spaniards and the French did too. In the late 1800's, when lead, coal and zinc were discovered, mines were opened.

Most of the mines were played out or became too costly to operate. Lands, once stripped bare by bulldozers and mechanical shovels, have been reclaimed. The deep pits, often surrounded by dense growths of man-made forests, are now ponds and lakes where anglers catch trophy-size fish.

A lone sentinel of mining's heyday in Southeast Kansas is "Big Brutus," a monstrous eleven million pound mechanical marvel. Sixteen stories tall, it could hold the equivalent of three railroad cars of rock and dirt with each scoop of its giant bucket.

Big Brutus belonged to The Pittsburg & Midway (P&M) Mining

Company and arrived in Kansas, in pieces, on one hundred fifty railroad cars. Assembly took fifty two P&M employees eleven months.

The mechanical shovel went to work in 1963, removing up to sixty nine feet of overburden covering coal seams. Other men and machinery moved in behind to extract the coal.

Three crews of three men each (shovel operator, ground man and oiler) operated Big Brutus 24-hours-a-day, seven days a week, for eleven years.

Although it was the world's second largest electric mining shovel when it was built, Big Brutus was never one for speed. It moved forward on its four pairs of crawlers at a snail-like .22 miles per hour. Four huge hydraulic jacks supported the crawler tracks and kept the machine in a level working position as it inched over the uneven pit floor.

In 1974 Big Brutus was abandoned near the community of West Mineral, eleven miles from where it had been assembled. The shovel sat idle until 1984 when P&M donated it and sixteen acres to a newly-formed non-profit organization, Big Brutus, Inc.

With the $100,000 P&M gave for restoration, volunteers cleaned and revamped the giant, and gave it a fresh coat of paint. Since 1985 it has been open to the public, dedicated to the mininng heritage of Southeast Kansas.

In 1933, Charlie Pichler lost his leg in a mining accident. To support him and their three children, his wife, Anne, sold sandwiches to other miners.

Fried chicken soon became a staple on Anne's menu. Potato salad and slaw were side dishes.

Anne retired in 1961 but her recipes didn't. Her delicious fried chicken is still served in several Chicken Annie's restaurants in the Pittsburg area. It's definitely not southern fried chicken, though. Everything is deep-fried in vegetable oil and has a garlic seasoning.

Chicken fried steak, onion rings, french fries and other items also are served.

Beef Brisket Cherisimo

1 (2-3 lb) Nutri-Beef Brisket

1½ tsp Carey Salt

½ tsp pepper

2 tbsp Grandma's Homestyle Mustard

3 tbsp brown sugar

1 bay leaf

1 small onion, thinly sliced

fresh spinach leaves and tomatoes
to garnish

Luscious Oven Barbecue Sauce:

½ cup vegetable oil

3 tbsp white vinegar

½ tsp salt

1 tsp sugar

½ tsp dry mustard

¼ tsp onion salt

¼ tsp paprika

¼ tsp dried oregano leaves

2 tsp garlic powder

1 tbsp finely chopped red bell pepper

1 tbsp liquid smoke

2 tbsp Worcestershire sauce

- Combine all ingredients for barbecue sauce in tightly covered container and shake well.
- Makes about ¾ cup sauce.
- Sprinkle beef with salt and pepper. Place in ungreased, oblong, covered 13″ x 9″ x 3″ roaster pan.
- Pour sauce over beef.
- Spread mustard on beef.
- Sprinkle brown sugar on beef; add bay leaf to sauce.
- Place sliced onion on and around brisket; cover.
- Bake in 300 degree oven for 3 hours.
- Remove brisket from roaster.
- Slice and serve.
- Garnish as desired with fresh spinach leaves and tomatoes.
- Serves 6.

Glazed Ham

½ cup Chautauqua Hills Apple
Cider Jelly

½ cup Dijon mustard

1 cup brown sugar

1 (6-7 lb) Solomon Valley Pride Ham

- Mix jelly, mustard and brown sugar together.
- Bake ham for 2½ hours at 325 degrees.
- Baste ham with mixture several times during baking.
- Serve additional glaze as condiment.
- Serves 10-12.

Prices are very reasonable and portions are ample, other reasons Chicken Annie's has become a Southeast Kansas dining tradition.

Fort Scott National Historic Site is Southeast Kansas' most visited attraction. It is America's only authentically restored military post from the period 1842-1853.

Militarily, things were quiet then. Only ten thousand people were in uniform. Many of the soldiers were charged with keeping peace along the undefined "Permanent Indian Frontier" between the established states of the Union and the unorganized territories to the west, including Kansas.

Fort Scott was established along the Kansas-Missouri border by the U.S. Army. It was originally garrisoned by two companies of dragoons, a special breed of colorfully dressed, heavily armed troops trained to fight on foot as well as on horseback.

The fort's primary purpose was to keep peace between the relocated Indians from the east, nomadic tribes and settlers. Strategically, it filled the gap between Fort Leavenworth to the north and Fort Gibson one hundred fifty miles to the south.

Most of Fort Scott's buildings were wood framed and Greek Revival in style. They were comfortable even by today's standards with high ceilings, walnut woodwork, porches and fireplaces. Eighteen of them have been restored to their original condition.

The visitors center was the post hospital. One of the two original wards has been refurbished. An exhibit of "modern medicine" of the mid-1880's shows what could happen to those unfortunate enough to become ill or disabled.

Other buildings include dragoon stables, infantry and dragoon barracks, post headquarters, a bakery, a powder magazine, a guardhouse and officer housing.

Captain Thomas Sword's quarters are the most elegantly furnished of

Smoked Pork Chops with Apple Raspberry Sauce

4 oz chunky applesauce

4 oz Flower of the Flames Raspberry BBQ Sauce

4 center cut Solomon Valley Pride Pork Loin Chops, 1" thick

Carey Salt

black pepper

fresh sage sprigs

- Preheat grill; position wire rack 4"-6" from heat. Combine applesauce and BBQ sauce; set aside.
- Rub both sides of chops with salt and pepper and place on rack.
- Place sage sprigs next to chops.
- Cover grill; cook, turning every 5 minutes.
- Serve pork chops with apple raspberry mixture.
- Serves 4.

Golden Stuffed Pork Chops

6 Solomon Valley Pride Pork Rib Chops, 1½" thick

1 small onion, finely chopped

2 tbsp butter

¾ cup cooked rice

1 cup shredded Alma Cheddar Cheese

1 tsp Worcestershire sauce

¼ tsp salt

⅛ tsp pepper

2 tbsp vegetable oil

- Using a small sharp knife, make a pocket in each pork chop. Cut into the center of the chop from the rib side, parallel to the rib bone and the surface of the chop.
- Sauté onion in butter until transparent; combine with rice, cheese, Worcestershire sauce, salt and pepper.
- Fill each pocket with 3 tbsp of rice mixture.
- Lightly brown chops in oil.
- Place on rack in roasting pan and cover securely with foil.
- Bake in 350 degree oven for 30 minutes.
- Uncover and bake for 30 minutes longer, or until done.
- Serves 6.

the officers' homes. It is often the focal point of activities, especially during the fort's popular Christmas candlelight tour.

Garrison life is depicted in other living history demonstrations. Costumed men and women role play to themes of barracks life; duties of stable personnel, the quartermaster and the laundress; and military drills and guard duty. Weapons demonstrations and mounted horse programs are always visitor pleasers.

Fort Scott also is an active participant in "Good Ol' Days," the annual June celebration in the city of the same name.

Unless you're an "old timer" who remembers an 1899 street fair, you've never seen anything to compare with the turn-of-the-century-like carnival. Calliopes, carousel organs and other instruments operated by electricity, hand and steam, give the "Good Ol' Days" celebration a flavor all its own.

Crafts, parades, entertainment and food are just as essential to Good Ol' Days as they are to other communities' festivals. Fort Scott goes all out to see that authentic foods are available to eager crowds. Snack items, like apple pie, old-fashioned caramel apples and barbecue, are a must.

Opportunities to see Fort Scott attractions, like the many Victorian homes and the beautiful U.S. National Cemetery, are made available to visitors during the celebration, and at other times during the year. The best way to tour the town is aboard the new motorized trackless trolley that was recently donated to the city.

Lawrence Strawder takes his three-week-old pig with him on nearly all the sales calls he makes. The pig has stayed in fine New York hotels, joined him for dinner at elegant restaurants and flown in the

Governor Mike's Beef Tenderloin

Kansas Beef recipe from Patti Hayden, wife of Governor Mike Hayden.

2 beef tenderloin strips (3½ lbs each)
soy sauce
Worcestershire sauce
garlic salt
salt
freshly ground pepper

Bearnaise Sauce:
½ cup sour cream
½ cup mayonnaise
2 tbsp tarragon vinegar
½ tsp salt
1 tsp tarragon leaves
½ tsp finely chopped shallots

- Combine the sauce ingredients and cover. Refrigerate.
- Tie together and brush beef tenderloin with soy sauce and Worcestershire sauce.
- Sprinkle with garlic salt, salt and pepper. Let stand at room temperature briefly.
- Bake the beef tenderloin for 45 minutes at 475 degrees.
- Let stand 5-7 minutes.
- While meat is standing, gently warm Bearnaise sauce.
- Slice tenderloin and serve immediately with warmed sauce.
- Serves 10-12.

Barbecued Buffalo

2-2½ lbs Butterfield's Buffalo Round Steak
½ cup chopped onion
1 medium clove garlic, minced
1 tbsp vegetable oil
1 cup ketchup
1 tsp celery flakes
3 tbsp brown sugar
¼ cup vinegar
1 tsp liquid smoke
2 tbsp Worcestershire sauce
red pepper sauce
garlic powder
salt
1 cup broth from cooked buffalo
hamburger buns or French bread slices

- Wrap buffalo steak in foil, folding edges to seal but leaving space for liquid to collect during cooking.
- Cook in slow cooker on low setting 8 hours, or until buffalo is fork tender. Shred meat.
- Mix together remaining ingredients except broth; heat. Add buffalo; mix well.
- Add enough broth for desired consistency. Heat to serving temperature.
- Serve over buns, open-face style, or bread.
- Serves 8-10.

passenger cabins of commercial aircraft.

Strawder's pig is a hand puppet, one of thousands his Country Critters company manufactures in Burlington, Kansas. The business sells its animals to more than five thousand stores in the United States and twenty foreign countries. Strawder uses only the finest materials available to ensure that his hand puppets are "the cutest most realistic puppets in the world." And, before being shipped, each one receives a personal grooming from Country Critters' resident beauticians.

The Burlington menagerie has become such a popular attraction with people wondering "how much is that little piggie in the window?" that free tours of the manufacturing facility are now offered Monday through Friday.

At five feet, four inches tall, Frederick Funston was not an intimidating person. He even tended to look a little frail. It was his inner strength and raw courage that made him a legend.

Funston grew up on a farm near Iola. In the 1890's, he joined many scientific expeditions to places such as the Dakota Badlands, Death Valley and Alaska. After a two-year stint in the Arctic, he canoed fifteen hundred miles down the Yukon River.

His research expeditions ceased while he was in Latin America. Funston decided to join the forces of the Cubans fighting for independence from Spain. He fought in twenty-two engagements until malaria forced him to return to the United States. But his brave adventures continued.

In 1901, Funston pulled off a daring ruse in the Philippines, sneaking into the Filipino army leader Emilio Aguinaldo's camp and capturing him. He received a Congressional Medal of Honor for his exploits and, at age 35, was elevated to the rank of brigadier general in the regular army.

Funston earned further recognition for his efforts to preserve law and order and assist the injured and homeless in San Francisco during the

Honey Glazed Pork Shoulder

4 lbs fresh Klema Locker Service Pork
Shoulder Roast

2 tbsp Sperry Apiaries Honey

1 tsp garlic salt

½ tsp ginger

½ tsp horseradish sauce

¼ tsp black pepper

- Place pork roast on rack in shallow baking pan.
- Roast in 325 degree oven for 2½ hours.
- Combine honey, garlic salt, ginger, horseradish sauce and pepper; brush over roast and bake 20 minutes longer.
- Serves 8-10.

Grilled Light Chicken

⅓ cup fresh lemon juice

¼ cup olive oil

2 cloves garlic, minced

1½ tbsp finely chopped David's Herbs
Rosemary

1½ tbsp finely chopped David's Herbs
Tarragon

½ tsp freshly ground black pepper

1 (3½ lb) fryer, split in half, skinned

1 (12 oz) btl Flower of the Flames Sugar
Free/Low Sodium BBQ Sauce

- In container, combine lemon juice, olive oil, garlic, rosemary, tarragon and pepper.
- Cover container tightly, shake vigorously.
- Pour marinade over top of chicken; turn to coat both sides.
- Cover and refrigerate 4 hours or overnight.
- Position wire rack 4"-6" from heat.
- Preheat grill.
- Place marinated chicken on rack.
- Grill 30-45 minutes, turning frequently.
- Brush lightly with sauce 20 minutes before serving.
- Serves 4.

1906 earthquake. In 1914 he commanded American troops along the Texas border as they fought the Mexican raider Pancho Villa.

Fightin' Fred Funston, as he was fondly known, died of a heart attack in 1917. William Allen White, a school classmate, wrote: he was "one of the most colorful figures in the American army from the day of Washington on down."

The general's home is located on U.S. 169 four miles north of Iola.

Martin Johnson was a handsome adventurer and explorer who came to Chanute, Kansas, to present a program and won the heart of his future wife, Osa.

The Johnsons, both native Kansans, traveled the world between 1917 and 1936 recording on film and in books the people and wildlife of remote areas from the South Seas to Africa. They were fearless . . . meeting with headhunters, and confronting wild animals with their cameras. They were also pioneers in the field of aerial photography and their aircraft incorporated never before used concepts that enabled them to land and take off in isolated fields and waterways.

The Martin & Osa Johnson Safari Museum in Chanute preserves the memorabilia of this legendary couple who, in their day, were as well known as any major movie star. Exhibits, like the African Tribal Culture Collection, include ceremonial carvings and domestic items representing over forty West African, and several East African, tribal groups. Some hands-on displays include a Dogon doorlock, a balafon and a narrow strip loom.

The museum also contains the Selsor Gallery of Fine Art with original watercolors, oil sketches and lithographs by leading natural history artists and illustrators.

Visitors can request to view a ten minute film of the Johnsons at work. The film shows headhunters and airplanes as seen through the Johnsons' camera lens.

Dill Chicken

1 (2-3 lb) chicken, cut in half
1 lemon, sliced
1 tsp Prairie Bounty Dill Seed
salt and pepper

- Place chicken, skin side up, in baking dish.
- Lift skin and insert lemon slices.
- Add water to baking dish to measure ½" deep.
- Sprinkle dill seed into water.
- Salt and pepper to taste.
- Bake 2 hours in 350 degree oven, or until done.
- Serves 4.

Rack of Lamb with Raspberry Mint Sauce

1½-2 lbs rack of lamb (rib roast)
¼ tsp oregano
2 tbsp chopped fresh Sunflower Organic Farm Rosemary
2 tsp salt
¼ tsp allspice
3 large cloves garlic, finely chopped
1 tsp black pepper
½ tsp dried leaf thyme
finely grated peel of 2 lemons
1 (12 oz) btl Flower of the Flames Raspberry BBQ Sauce
3 tbsp mint sauce
apple and pecan wood chips to grill

- Have butcher trim rack of lamb, removing all visible fat and thin flap of meat on the end of the rib.
- Also have the butcher cut through the chime bone.
- Cut and scrape meat from between long rib bones, leaving 2"-3" of clean bone protruding.
- Cover exposed bone with a double layer of foil to keep from burning.
- In a small bowl, combine oregano, rosemary, salt, allspice, garlic, pepper, thyme and lemon peel.
- Rub mixture over surface of lamb; cover, refrigerate at least 2 hours.
- Place lamb on grill at opposite end from coals; smoke for about 1½-2 hours; fire should be medium.
- Mix BBQ and mint sauce in a pan, and simmer for 10 minutes.
- Serve warm with lamb.
- Serves 4.

Oil has helped build Kansas. Huge reservoirs of the "black gold" have been found under its fertile soils and tapped for nearly a century.

Results from the first well drillings were hardly cause for optimism, however. Until 1892, drillers came up with dry holes or wells with too little oil to be commercially successful. Eastern experts, commenting on failed attempts to find fossil fuel in Kansas and other western states, bragged that they "could drink all of the oil that would be discovered west of the Mississippi."

In 1891, several prominent citizens of Neodesha invited former Pennsylvania oil man William M. Mills to drill wells in their town. Their hope was that he would come up with natural gas to supply the city's needs. His research determined that the best place to drill was a garden plot belonging to T.J. Norman, a local blacksmith.

By November, 1892, at a depth of slightly under eight hundred feet, the steel bit chopped into an oil sand. Eight months later three hundred seventy-one barrels of oil had been pumped from the well. The average daily output settled at twelve barrels.

Norman No. 1 was the first commercial well in the Mid-Continent region. It pumped on a vast field that was producing over half of the nation's oil supply by 1919. The well continued to do so until the late 1930's.

A replica of the Norman No. 1 wooden derrick is a part of Neodesha's Historical Oil Museum & Park. It stands sixty-seven feet high and has a twenty-two foot square base. Some of the well's original equipment, including the bullwheel, is displayed on the actual site, now a National Historic Landmark.

Distinguished American playwright William Motter Inge was born in Independence, Kansas. His work "Picnic" earned a Pulitzer Prize. "Splendor In The Grass" won him an Academy Award.

Inge had other Broadway successes that made him legendary in

Grilled Chef's Prime

2-4 lbs boneless Lone Pine Farms Pork
Rib-End Roast

- Prepare medium hot coals in covered grill, banking coals on sides of grill.
- Place drip pan in center of grill bed.

Basting Sauce:

¾ cup chili sauce
¼ cup cider vinegar
1 tsp dry mustard

- Mix together basting sauce ingredients.
- Place pork on grill over drip pan.
- Close grill; roast pork for 45 minutes-1½ hours, basting every 10-15 minutes with basting sauce.
- Remove pork from grill when internal temperature reaches 155-160 degrees.
- Serves 8-12.

Rolled Round Steak

2 (4 oz) cans mushrooms, minced
2 tbsp Rabbit Creek Bacon-Flavored
Onion Dip Mix
2 tsp Worcestershire sauce
1 (2 lb) Hoseney's Round Steak,
tenderized

- Combine mushrooms, dip mix and Worcestershire sauce.
- Spread on round steak.
- Roll up steak, jellyroll fashion.
- Tie roll in 3-4 places with string, and place seam side down on a foil covered, 13" x 9" x 2" baking pan.
- Bake in 350 degree oven for 1½ hours, or until done.
- Serves 6.

writing circles. "Come Back, Little Sheba," The Dark At The Top Of The Stairs" and "Spendor In The Grass" continue to be performed today.

Laura Ingalls Wilder made Independence famous when her autobiography depicting happiness and hardship on the Kansas plains at the turn of the century, was made into a television series. "Little House on the Prairie" became a prime time hit.

As the program gained in popularity, people from across the nation traveled to the Kurtis farm thirteen miles southwest of the city, where Laura had lived from 1869 to 1870.

"Early visitors were disappointed not to find any of the homestead still standing," Bill Kurtis said, "so, we decided to construct a cabin resembling the original one Pa Ingalls had built at this location."

Over one hundred volunteers from Independence, and nearby, took on the building of the cabin. Much of the material and logs came from the farm. It was dedicated July 2, 1977.

The first modern-day proof that the Ingalls lived in Montgomery County was discovered when the Kansas State Historical Society located the name "Ingles" in the 1870 census of Rutland Township. Although the surname was misspelled, the first names of the family members were correct; C.P. Ingles was listed as a 34-year-old carpenter, his wife Caroline, 30, and their three daughters Mary, 5, Laura, 3, and Carrie, 2½ years.

The census was taken by Assistant Marshal Asa Hairgrove, who covered the entire township in two days. Rutland Township is eight miles wide by nine miles long. Hairgrove listed one hundred thirty-two residences in the township. The fact that the Ingalls' name was misspelled is a good sign he didn't actually call at the Ingalls' home. Additionally, Carrie's age was inaccurately recorded. She was really just two weeks old.

Many of the landmarks Laura Ingalls Wilder mentioned in her autobiography can still be seen on the Kurtis farm, and nearby, today. The

Tex-Mex Chicken

¼ cup milk

1 cup HearTland Mill® Yellow
Corn Meal

4 tbsp Rabbit Creek Spicey
Mexican Dip Mix

1 (3-3½ lb) whole chicken, cut in pieces

¼ cup melted butter or margarine

- Preheat oven to 375 degrees, or prepare outdoor grill for barbecuing.
- Pour milk into pie plate.
- On waxed paper, combine corn meal and dip mix; mix well.
- Dip chicken pieces into milk, then into corn meal mixture, coating all sides.
- Place, skin side up, in large roasting pan; drizzle with melted butter.
- Bake 45 minutes.
- If cooking chicken on grill, use the indirect method: cover the grill with foil first, then place the chicken on it.
- Grill 30-45 minutes, turning twice.
- Serves 6.

Raspberry Mustard Glazed Pork Roast

1 (12 oz) btl Flower of the Flames
Raspberry BBQ Sauce

2 tbsp finely grated orange peel

¼ cup fresh orange juice

¼ cup Grandma's Homestyle Mustard

1 tsp minced gingerroot
or ½ tsp ginger

½ tsp salt

¼ tsp cayenne

3½-4 lbs boneless Solomon Valley Pride
Pork Top Loin Roast, tied

apple wood chips to grill

- In small bowl, combine first 7 ingredients; set aside.
- Preheat grill for indirect cooking.
- Place wire rack 4"-6" over drip pan; place roast on rack.
- Cover grill, open vents slightly.
- Cook roast 45 minutes and turn.
- Add briquets and chips to fire as needed.
- Baste with glaze every 10 minutes.
- Cook for another 45 minutes, or until pork has a slight tinge of pink when cut at thickest part.
- Remove from grill, wrap in plastic film; let stand for 10 minutes.
- Serves 8.

well, the buffalo wallow, Walnut Creek and the bluffs to the north of the homestead, authenticate the site. Mr. Edward's homestead mentioned in the books, is located one mile northeast of the site on the same farm. Dr. George Tann's farm adjoins the site on the north, separated by Highway 75, and his grave can be found in Mount Hope Cemetery in Independence.

Little House on the Prairie, Inc., is a non-profit organization that administers the historic attraction. Its purpose is twofold. "We want to encourage children to read not only the 'Little House' books," Kurtis said, "but other books as well, and to learn to enjoy reading. Our second purpose is to encourage people, especially children, to live by the principles laid down by Laura Ingalls Wilder in her writings: 'It is best to be honest and truthful; to make the most of what we have; to be happy with simple pleasures and to be cheerful and have courage when things go wrong.'"

Two other buildings are also located in the "Little House" park. One is the Sunny Side Schoolhouse, which has been restored with original desks and chairs, to show children how school used to be conducted. The other building is the Wayside Post Office. According to Kurtis, it dates back almost to the turn-of-the-century.

As the Independence community has been caught up in the "Little House" spirit so has Kurtis' wife, Wilma. She and Anita Gold, antiques editor of the *Chicago Tribune,* co-authored the book, "Prairie Recipes and Kitchen Antiques." The material is centered around the 1870's era.

Little House on the Prairie's future as a Kansas tourist attraction will be low-keyed, just as it is today. "We want to keep it simple," Kurtis emphasized, "the way it was."

F ormer Independence Mayor Charles Kerr occupies an obscure place in history. In 1988, the Chicago Cubs were the last major league baseball team to illuminate their stadium for night games—a lighted Wrigley Field was a worldwide media event.

In contrast, the first professional baseball game ever played under

Ginger Lime Pork

1 lb Lone Pine Farms Pork Tenderloin,
partially frozen until firm

12 fresh broccoli flowerets

4 medium Bismarck Gardens Carrots,
julienned

2 tbsp vegetable oil, divided

6 tbsp Fields of Fair Dry White Wine,
divided

2 tbsp lime juice

⅛ tsp salt

⅛ tsp black pepper

1 tsp finely grated fresh ginger

½ tsp finely grated lime peel

- Cut pork diagonally into ¼″ thick pieces; slice again into thin strips; set aside.
- Heat 1 tbsp oil in large skillet; add carrots.
- Cook 5 minutes, stirring often.
- Add broccoli; cook 1 minute.
- Add 1 tbsp wine; cover and cook until vegetables are crisp tender, 4-5 minutes; remove.
- Heat remaining oil in skillet. Add pork; cook and stir until no longer pink, 3-4 minutes. Lower heat.
- Combine rest of wine, lime juice, salt, pepper, ginger and lime peel.
- Add to skillet; heat 2 minutes.
- Return vegetables to skillet; toss lightly; heat 1 minute.
- Serves 4.

Barbecue Ribs

6-8 lbs Oakland Pork Rib Slabs

½ tsp salt

½ tsp pepper

1 (18 oz) btl Curley's Barbecue Sauce

- Place rib slabs in 9″ x 13″ cake pan. Salt and pepper; cover pan with foil.
- Bake in 300 degree oven for 3 hours, or until tender.
- Place rib slabs on hot charcoal grill approximately 10 minutes on each side.
- Turn ribs; baste generously with sauce.
- Grill 1-2 minutes before turning ribs.
- Baste.
- Serves 6-8.

permanent illumination drew little attention ouside of Kerr's hometown, where it was held, and some neighboring Kansas communities. The year was 1930.

Attendance at Southeast Kansas City's Producers Park had been sluggish. Kerr, an avid baseball fan, and the Independence Producers' owners, were unhappy. The Mayor thought larger crowds might be attracted to games if they were played at night.

Fifty and sixty-foot poles, with lights attached, were erected at the park. The ninety thousand watts of light they produced would, according to the *Independence Reporter* newspaper, make the field "lighter than daylight and enable the players to go to the far corners of the field and get them (baseballs)."

That first night game pitted the Independence Producers against the then-famed House of David team from Michigan. The feared Michiganers were, according to the Reporter, "members of a cult which prevents them from cutting their beards or hair, and that alone has kept many members from making the trip to the big show (major leagues)."

The score, for the record, was 9-1 in favor of the Producers.

Under a headline that proclaimed "Glow In Heavens Visible for Miles," the Reporter stated: "Never before has a baseball club started the season with floodlights furnishing the illumination for the spectacular plays which are manufactured in a professional baseball factory." Further, it said, "Independence is thus leading the world in the plan which experts say will ultimately result in adoption (of lights) by practically every minor league baseball team in the world."

Twelve hundred spectators showed up for that first night game but they never could seem, said the Reporter, "to get settled down to the fact that the ball, traveling away from the stands, was held so true by the illumination of the floodlights, that it appears to be hanging in mid-air."

I t sounded like a good plan at the time to the gang of desperados. They would ride into Coffeyville, Kansas, split up, and rob two banks

Roulade of Pork with Jalapenos and Cheese

1½ lbs boneless Solomon Valley Pride Pork Loin

¾ cup grated jalapeno cheese

¼ cup diced mild chilies

1½ cups milk

1 egg

flour, as needed

1½ cups dry bread crumbs

2 tbsp vegetable oil

1 cup sliced onion

1 tsp minced garlic

⅛ tsp grated nutmeg

⅛ tsp cinnamon

1 cup Fuego Picante Sauce

1 cup chopped tomatoes

1 cup vegetable oil

- Cut pork loin into 6 slices; butterfly and pound thin.
- Sprinkle grated cheese on each slice; top with chilies.
- Roll slices tightly. Chill until firm.
- Mix together milk and egg.
- Dip rolls in flour and shake well.
- Dip in egg mixture and then into bread crumbs. Shake well and chill.
- Preheat oven to 350 degrees.
- Heat 2 tbsp oil.
- Sauté onion and garlic until golden.
- Add nutmeg and cinnamon; stir 1 minute.
- Add picante sauce and tomatoes.
- Simmer 10 minutes; remove from heat.
- Heat 1 cup oil to medium high; add pork rolls. Cook until golden.
- Transfer to baking pan. Bake for 10 minutes.
- Serve with additional heated picante sauce.
- Serves 6.

Fruited Smoked Pork Chops

1 medium red Valley Pride Apples Cooking Apple, sliced

1 large pear, sliced

1 small lime, thinly sliced

2 tbsp butter

1 tbsp brown sugar

4 Lone Pine Farms Smoked Pork Chops

- Sauté fruit in butter 2 minutes; stir in brown sugar, cook until bubbly.
- Remove from heat, cover; keep warm while cooking chops.
- Broil chops 5 minutes on each side.
- Serve chops covered with fruit.
- Serves 4.

Sunset over Kansas

Lamb Roast with Apricot Glaze

4-5 lbs boneless leg of lamb roast

1 cup apricot preserves

1/3 cup lemon juice

1 (3 oz) pkg cream cheese, softened

5 slices Duis Delights Bacon, cooked and crumbled

1 (8 oz) can apricot halves

- Place roast, fat side up, on rack in open roasting pan.
- Combine apricot preserves and lemon juice.
- Spread half of the preserve mixture over the lamb.
- Roast in 325 degree oven for 2½-3 hours, basting continuously.
- Shape cream cheese into 8 balls and roll in crumbled bacon.
- Place cheese balls in center of apricot halves; use apricot halves to garnish roast.
- Serve remaining apricot glaze as a sauce for lamb.
- Serves 12.

Easy Fried Catfish

1 cup Steffen's Buttermilk

1 tsp salt

1 tsp pepper

6 pan-dressed Culver Fish Farm Catfish

1½ cups HearTland Mill® Corn Meal

½ cup self-rising flour

6 cups vegetable oil

- Mix buttermilk, salt and pepper in deep container.
- Add fish and turn to coat evenly.
- Marinate 4-6 hours or overnight; drain.
- Mix corn meal and flour; roll catfish in meal mixture, coating evenly.
- Fry fish, a few at a time, in deep oil at 370 degrees until fish is golden brown.
- Serves 6.

simultaneously. The day they picked to do this was October 7, 1892.

The robbers counted on the element of surprise, and firepower from their guns, for success. But they didn't count on the determination of the local citizens to protect their interests.

As the robbers made to escape from the Condon Bank and the First National Bank they entered "Death Alley" as it is now known locally. Unarmed citizens, hearing of the commotion, took guns from the hardware store and challenged the thieves. When the battle was over, four members of the infamous Dalton Gang, and four defenders, were dead. Of the outlaws, only Emmett Dalton survived.

The bodies of the fatally wounded Dalton gang were taken to the Coffeyville Jail. Today, visitors to the jail hear a recording that retells the story of the robbers' plot and their demise.

The Dalton Museum in Coffeyville features personal effects of gang members plus other historical items. Photos of the dead outlaws, laid out together as if they were trophies, represent the law of the Old West, where bad guys never really won.

The incident is remembered each October during "Dalton Defenders Days." Local amateur actors portray the good guys and the bad guys.

W.P. Brown came to Coffeyville from Independence and settled near present day Seventh and Maple streets. He earned his wealth in the natural gas business.

No self-respecting man of means would live in an ordinary house in the early 1900's, and Brown was no exception. He contracted with some Kansas City architects to design a home for him. It was completed in 1906 at the modest sum of $125,000. Brown owned Coffeyville's lumber yard and he was able to wholesale himself the building materials.

There are fifteen rooms on the main and second floors and nine have fireplaces, all different. Some rooms have original hand-painted canvas wall coverings. Chandeliers are both gas and electric powered. Most of

Italian Paprika Filets

1 cup oats

⅓ cup grated Parmesan cheese

1 tsp crushed Italian seasoning

½ tsp paprika

¼ cup skim milk

1 egg white, slightly beaten

1 lb fresh Culver Fish Farm Catfish Filets

2 tbsp melted butter

1 tbsp fresh snipped Pickett's Gardens Parsley

- Lightly oil rack or broiler pan.
- Grind oats in blender or food processor about 1 minute; stir.
- In shallow dish, combine dry ingredients.
- In another shallow dish, combine milk and egg white.
- Coat filets with oat mixture; shake off excess.
- Dip into egg mixture; coat again with oat mixture.
- Place onto pan; drizzle with butter.
- Broil about 4" from heat 3½-4½ minutes, or until golden brown.
- Top filets with parsley.
- Serves 4.

Oven Fried Catfish
"Celebrate! Kansas Food" Contest Winner

2 slices cracked wheat bread

¼ cup melted Steffen's Butter

1½ tbsp fresh lemon juice

½ tsp sugar

¼ tsp pepper

¼ tsp paprika

1 tbsp chopped David's Herbs Fresh Basil

⅛ tsp garlic powder

½ tsp Carey Salt

1 lb Culver Fish Farm Catfish, cut into 4 pieces

- Lightly grease a 7" x 11" shallow glass baking dish.
- Tear bread slices into pieces and place in food processor.
- Process into fine crumbs, set aside.
- Combine butter, lemon juice, sugar, pepper, paprika, basil, garlic and salt.
- Dip catfish pieces in butter mixture; roll in the bread crumbs.
- Arrange catfish in a single layer in prepared dish.
- Spoon the remaining butter mixture over the fish.
- Bake, uncovered, in 450 degree oven for 15 minutes, or until fish flakes easily with fork.
- Serves 4.

the furniture is original and is in excellent condition.

Leaded Tiffany glass accents the main doorway and a signed Tiffany chandelier in the dining room is believed to have been personally hung by the designer.

The third floor contains a fabulous ballroom where numerous parties were enjoyed. The floor is hardwood. The ceilings are hand-painted. Lampshades are made of crystal. Alcoves for smoking open out onto roofs above pillared porches.

The mansion was purchased by the Coffeyville Historical Society from Brown's daughter in 1973 and is open for public viewing. It is well worth a visit.

N estled in a grove of trees on the picturesque banks of Spring River, is Riverton's locally famous Spring River Inn. The Joplin, Missouri, Country Club built the building in 1905.

A huge stone fireplace inside the lobby draws admiring glances. It is the work of real craftsmen. See if you can find the beer bottles imbedded in the mortar for reasons only the workers knew.

The famous Spring River Inn smorgasbord is the work of masters, too. Everything is made from scratch, on the premises. Instant mashed potatoes? Proprietors Judy and Raymond Birk would not think of it.

Since 1952 a thirty-five foot serving table has been stocked with a tempting array of delicious foods. Some items, like fried chicken, are always served. After all, it's a Southeast Kansas tradition. Fried shrimp is also a regular.

The Inn's squaw bread and cinnamon pull-a-parts are legendary in the region. Desserts border on decadent.

There is no ordering from the menu at the restaurant because there isn't a menu. Smorgasbord only. If anyone goes away hungry, though, it's their own fault. The selection is good and there is always plenty to go around.

Catfish Parmesan

6 skinned, pan-dressed Culver Fish Farm Catfish, fresh or frozen

2 cups dry bread crumbs

¾ cup Parmesan cheese

¼ cup chopped David's Herbs Fresh Parsley

1 tsp paprika

½ tsp leaf oregano

¼ tsp leaf basil

½ tsp pepper

2 tsp salt

¾ cup melted butter

lemon wedges

- Thaw frozen fish.
- Clean, wash and dry fish.
- Combine bread crumbs, Parmesan cheese, parsley, paprika, oregano, basil, pepper and salt.
- Dip catfish in melted butter and roll in crumb mixture.
- Arrange fish in well greased baking dish. Bake in 375 degree oven 30-35 minutes or until fish flakes easily when tested with a fork.
- Garnish with lemon wedges.
- Serves 6.

Charcoal Grilled Catfish

6 medium Culver Fish Farm Catfish

salt and pepper

2 tbsp vegetable oil

6 slices Hickory Point Bacon

- Filet fish lengthwise.
- Salt and pepper well.
- Brush both sides of fish with vegetable oil.
- Wrap bacon around each piece.
- Place in a wire rack and grill over charcoal fire until bacon and fish are done.
- Serves 6.

D r. Samuel Crumbine, a brilliant physician serving as the first secretary of the Kansas Board of Health, and Frank H. Rose, a school teacher from Weir City, were the two men behind one of the most effective disease-fighting products of this century.

Just an inch over five feet tall, Crumbine was to become a giant in the public health field. He had been convinced by his friend Dr. Victor C. Vaughan, in 1905, that flies were among the principal offenders in transmitting typhoid bacteria. He searched for a way to eliminate them.

A year later, at a Western League baseball game where Crumbine was in attendance, Topeka was trailing arch rival Wichita in the ninth inning. The local club had a man on third base with just one out. The crowd began to chant for the batter to hit a sacrifice fly ball and enable the base runner to score.

One man broke with the crowd and began yelling "swat the ball, swat the ball."

The doctor took an envelope from his pocket and jotted down the slogan, "swat the fly." His enthusiasm for the idea was such that he left the game early and never knew who won.

But credit for the tool that became most popular for eradicating flies belongs to school teacher Rose.

Rose's Boy Scout troop wanted to help in Crumbine's public campaign so they began cleaning the town. Trash was hauled to the local dump and burned. Then the teacher bought a roll of screen wire and a bundle of yardsticks. The Scouts cut the yardsticks and measured the wire into small squares.

The shortened measuring sticks became handles for the screens and the first of what Rose called "fly bats" had been made. They were distributed door-to-door to the citizens of Weir City.

Rose also presented one of his inventions to Dr. Crumbine. The physician was delighted with it but said, instead of calling it a fly bat, "let's call it a fly swatter."

SOUTH CENTRAL KANSAS

S outh Central Kansas is Amish buggies and jet airplanes, Swedish folk dancers and Indians, covered wagons and spacecraft. It is the beautiful Flint Hills, golden wheat fields, and the Gypsum Hills that would make you swear you were in Arizona red rock country. It is rural, it is cosmopolitan. The state's largest city, Wichita, is located here. So are some of Kansas' most outstanding visitor attractions.

Hutchinson, Kansas seems an unlikely site for an internationally known space museum. The city is located in America's heartland, well over one thousand miles from either of America's two spaceports in California and Florida. Yet, the Kansas Cosmophere and Space Center, an unusually designed solar-paneled building on the local community college campus, contains a collection of space artifacts that rivals exhibits at the Kennedy Space Center and the Smithsonian Institution.

The largest single display in the Hutchinson museum is a full-size moonscape that includes a mockup of a lunar lander, a made-for-television lunar rover vehicle, and astronaut mannequins. The lunar lander was used by the NBC television network to demonstrate maneuvers that were simultaneously taking place on the moon. The lunar rover vehicle was built for the TV mini-series "Space." Spacesuits the "astronauts" wear are from the Cosmosphere's collection, the largest in the United States.

Encased nearby, is moon rock brought back to earth by the *Apollo 11* astronauts.

How did Hutchinson, Kansas obtain all of this?

A grassroots effort led by Executive Director Max Ary and local philanthropist Patty Carey raised more than two and one-half million dollars for the science center. The city, Reno County and local foundations, organizations and companies contributed heavily to the project.

While the fund-drive was in progress, Ary was in contact with National Aeronautics and Space Administration (NASA) officials in order to procure significant space artifacts such as rocket engines, space suits and spacecraft. They authorized him to cannibalize some abandoned launch pads at the Kennedy Space Center, which he did. He also returned from Florida with the largest rocket engine ever manufactured—the F-1 which generated thirty-million horsepower on *Saturn 5* launch vehicles. The engine was restored and placed on a pedestal in front of the completed museum.

The museum has three distinct sections. The one hundred seven-seat OMNIMAX Theatre, with its forty-four-foot tilted dome screen, is the smallest of its kind in the world. Everything inside, however, is state-of-the-art including a more than $500,000 six-channel sound system that provides a remarkable sense of "being there." Don't sit near the front or you'll miss a lot. The best seats are in the center of the auditorium, near the top.

The Planetarium theater projects a simulated view of the nighttime sky onto a domed viewing surface in order to take the audience on journeys into space and time. The theater is primarily used as a teaching tool to introduce astronomy, earth motions, and related science topics to students.

VEGETABLES

An autumn road

Exhibits in the Hall of Space chronologically trace man's quest to reach the stars, beginning with American physicist Robert Goddard's launch of a liquid fueled rocket in the 1920's. The rocket achieved an altitude of only forty-one feet. Although the rocket was destroyed, Cosmosphere technicians have exactingly built a replica using Goddard's original blueprints.

Museum staff members are proud that their self-taught restoration experts have made the Kansas center the only one, aside from the Smithsonian and NASA museums, to have in its collection a complete set of flight-ready spacecraft. Among them are the backup to *Explorer I*, the first American satellite to achieve orbit.

Just as rare are the small Mercury backup capsule and an *Apollo-Soyuz* trainer. Only six Mercury missions were flown and just a few backup capsules were saved. Visitors are amazed at how small the cabin is. It took astronauts, in their spacesuits, fifteen minutes to get inside.

The *Apollo-Soyuz* craft was used by United States astronauts and Soviet cosmonauts preparing for their joint mission in the 1970's.

Visitors also can view Gemini craft, an engine from one of the first German Luftwaffe jets, and a rare, full-sized replica of the first Soviet satellite, *Sputnik*.

The Cosmosphere recently acquired U.S. Army Redstone and U.S. Air Force *Titan I* rockets, plus two World War II German V-1 and V-2 rockets ("V" for Vengeance). They bring the center closer to its goal of having a complete collection of the early rockets.

The museum had the most difficulty in obtaining a trenching scoop from the unmanned *Surveyor 3* spacecraft. NASA sent three Surveyor probes to the moon to test planned techniques for manned landings on the lunar surface. *Apollo 12*'s crew used the last one as a target for a pinpoint landing. The astronauts returned home with the scoop which had been on the moon for thirty months . . . the first man-made object returned to earth after long-term exposure to the hostile environment of space.

Ary claims the Cosmosphere is not just a museum but a space

Stir-Fried Asparagus

3 tbsp butter

1 medium onion, peeled and chopped

1-2 lbs Pendleton's Fresh Asparagus, cut into 1½" pieces

2 tbsp water

6-10 Toto Cure of Kansas Mushrooms

salt

- Melt butter in frying pan.
- Sauté onion until transparent.
- Add asparagus and stir-fry 1 minute, reserving tips.
- Add water; cover and steam for 1 minute.
- Add asparagus tips and mushrooms. Stir until well blended.
- Cover and steam for 1 minute, until mushrooms are thoroughly heated and asparagus is bright green and still crisp. Salt to taste.
- Serves 4-6.

Cauliflower Walnut Casserole
"Celebrate! Kansas Food" Contest Winner

1 medium head cauliflower

1¼ cups Steffen's Sour Cream

1 tbsp all-purpose flour

1 cup grated Alma Cheddar Cheese

2 tsp seasoned chicken stock base

1 tsp dry mustard

¼ cup chopped Carden Pecans

¼ cup fine dry bread crumbs

1 tbsp melted Steffen's Butter

1 tsp crumbled dried marjoram leaves

¼ tsp onion salt

- Cook cauliflower in 1" salted water until tender; drain and place half the cauliflower in 9" x 13" baking dish.
- Combine sour cream, flour, cheese, chicken stock base and mustard.
- Pour half of sauce over cauliflower; reserve remaining sauce.
- Top with remaining cauliflower and sauce.
- Combine pecans, bread crumbs, butter, marjoram and onion salt.
- Sprinkle over casserole.
- Bake in 400 degree oven 15-20 minutes.
- Serves 4-6.

resource center that strives to put people in touch with the vitality and excitement of the evolving story of man's journey to the stars.

"We're preserving and displaying space history as it is made," he notes, "so that the voyages of today may be better understood tomorrow."

In so doing, many of the exhibits at the Kansas center are "hands on."

A lunar module cockpit faithfully restored to replicate the series of events necessary for moon landings, is one of the most popular of these "do touch" items. Visitors can select any one of the six lunar landings that U.S. space crews made, and see what they saw as they touched down. The experience is authenticated by recordings of the excited astronauts as they neared their objective.

An astronaut data bank profiles every American launched into space. Through computer selection, Cosmosphere visitors can find out which missions each American flew or trivia such as food likes and dislikes.

Exploration of the unknown sometimes results in tragedy as the recent *Challenger* explosion demonstrated. A touching memorial at the Cosmosphere honors that crew, and members of *Apollo 1* who died in flames on the launch pad. It serves as a permanent reminder that pioneering is not accomplished without some degree of risk.

Astronauts are regular visitors to the Kansas facility. As a testament to its quality, and the professionalism of the staff, the space heroes frequently donate personal mementos of their space travel to to the center.

Included in the newest additions to the Cosmosphere's collection of artifacts is a Soviet spacesuit worn by Svetlana Savitskaya, the first woman to walk in space. It was obtained when executive director Ary jokingly told a friend, who was going to Moscow, to pick one up for him.

The Soviets were receptive to the idea and agreed to trade the spacesuit for a twenty-year old backup suit from an Apollo flight. The spacesuit, the first permitted to be exhibited in the West, is the only Soviet suit on display anywhere that has actually been "Flown."

"Even the spacesuits the Soviets exhibit in their own museums are backups," says Ary. "This is the genuine article. Savitskaya used it on

Smokey Baked Beans

1 (16 oz) can pork and beans, drained

1 small onion, chopped

½ green bell pepper, chopped

½ cup brown sugar

¾ cup Kingsfords Original K Barbeque Sauce

- Mix beans, chopped onion and green pepper.
- Add brown sugar and barbeque sauce. Mix well.
- Bake in 350 degree oven for 1½ hours.
- Serves 6-8.

Mexican Seasoned Rice

1 cup uncooked white rice

3 tbsp Rabbit Creek Spicey Mexican Dip Mix

2 cups water

1 tbsp butter

- In medium saucepan, bring all ingredients to boil.
- Cover and simmer 20 minutes, or until rice is tender.
- Serves 6.

Scalloped Potatoes

4 cups thickly sliced Britt's Garden Acres Potatoes

1 cup sliced Britt's Garden Acres Carrots

¼ cup chopped onion

¼ cup chopped green pepper

1 cup cubed Solomon Valley Pride Boneless Ham

½ cup shredded Pioneer Cheddar Cheese

Sauce:

2 tbsp melted butter

2 tbsp all-purpose flour

¾ tsp salt

¼ tsp pepper

2 cups milk

- To make sauce, mix together butter and flour; add salt, pepper and milk.
- Cook, stirring constantly, until thickened; set aside.
- In a buttered 2 qt casserole, layer half of all vegetables and ham.
- Cover with half of sauce; repeat.
- Sprinkle cheese over casserole. Bake, covered, at 350 degrees for 1 hour.
- Uncover, bake additional 10 minutes.
- Serves 6-8.

both of her missions."

The Kansas Cosmosphere and Space Center charges no admission fee. There is a charge for planetarium showings and OMNIMAX theater presentations.

Food and beverages aren't allowed in the facility but the gift shop has astronaut ice cream for sale. Try it. Don't be fooled by the small size of the package, a single serving will be more than enough for a group to pass around.

Nestled in the Smoky Hill River Valley is a small community that visiting Swedes claim is "more Swedish than Sweden." The town of Lindsborg, "Little Sweden U.S.A."

There's no mistaking that the majority of Lindsborg's 3,200 citizens are of Scandinavian descent and are proud of their roots. Old World facades adorn almost every business in town. Bright red wooden Dala horses—typical examples of Swedish folk art—are prominently displayed in front of most residences. Restaurants and bakeries prepare Swedish staples and delicacies daily. Even the local college's athletic teams are known as the Fighting Swedes.

Lindsborg celebrates three major festivals: St. Lucia in December, Midsommardag (Midsummer's Day) in June and Svensk Hyllningsfest, the largest and most popular of the community's celebrations. The latter is held every odd numbered year in October. Townspeople of all ages don their finest Swedish costumes and dance and sing to authentic Swedish music while appreciative visitors look on.

But Lindsborg is interesting every day. Shops featuring Swedish imports and locally made goods, art galleries, historical attractions and fine dining establishments provide a delightful Scandinavian sampler.

Hemslojd, or the Dala Horse Factory, is one of Lindsborg's most popular shops. You can see Ken Sjogren make the brightly painted wooden plaques which originated in the Swedish province of Dalarna in the 1840's.

Long quiet winter evenings in nineteenth-century Sweden and the

Blackeyed Peas and Rice

1 (6.75 oz) pkg Olde Westport
Cajun Rice Mix

2 tbsp olive oil

1 bell pepper, chopped

1 small onion, chopped

2 stalks celery, minced

½ lb Krehbiel's Ham, cubed

2 (16 oz) cans blackeyed peas, drained

1 bay leaf, crumbled

1 tsp Olde Westport Cajun Seasoning

water, as needed

- Prepare rice mix according to pkg directions.
- Meanwhile, add olive oil to skillet and sauté bell pepper, onion and celery until crisp tender.
- In a large saucepan, add rice, vegetables, ham, blackeyed peas, bay leaf and Cajun seasonings. Stir in water as needed.
- Cover pan and heat on low, 5 minutes.
- Serves 6.

Sweet-Sour Green Beans and Carrots
"Celebrate! Kansas Food" Contest Winner

1 cup chopped Bismarck Gardens Carrots

1 (9 oz) pkg frozen cut green beans

2 slices Roepke's Processing Plant Bacon

1 medium Britt's Garden Acres Onion,
sliced

1 Champlin's Orchard Apple, peeled,
cored and sliced

2 tbsp vinegar

1 tbsp sugar

½ tsp Carey Salt

- In saucepan, cook carrots until tender.
- Add green beans and cook until tender; drain.
- In a skillet, cook bacon until crisp; drain, reserving 1 tbsp of drippings.
- Crumble bacon; set aside.
- Sauté onion in reserved drippings until tender but not brown.
- Add apple, vinegar, sugar and salt.
- Cover and cook just until apples are tender, 3-4 minutes.
- Add carrots and beans; heat thoroughly.
- Sprinkle bacon on top.
- Serves 4-6.

*"You'll like Kansas . . . it's the very
perfection of prairie country—not flat, not
boggy, but gently swelling, with rich valleys
and sloping everywhere. Eden sloped, you
remember—'beautiful as the garden of the
angels upon the slopes in Eden.'"*

Henry King
Atlantic Monthly

Touched by a rainbow, Jefferson County

Glazed Carrots

4 cups sliced Bismarck Gardens Carrots	▪ Steam carrots until fork tender.
1 cup Chautauqua Hills Apple Cider Jelly	▪ Remove from steamer and place in saucepan; add jelly. Heat until jelly is dissolved.
	▪ Serves 8.

Zucchini and Corn

¼ cup butter	▪ Melt butter in large skillet; add vegetables, salt and dip mix.
4 cups sliced King's Orchard Zucchini	
1½ cups fresh King's Orchard Corn	▪ Cover and cook over medium heat 10-12 minutes, stirring occasionally.
½ cup chopped onion	
⅓ cup chopped green pepper	▪ Serves 4-6.
½ tsp salt	
1 tbsp Rabbit Creek Bacon Onion Dip Mix	

Superb Pea Casserole

½ lb Toto Cure of Kansas Mushrooms, sliced	▪ Sauté mushrooms in butter; drain mushrooms, reserving liquid.
4 tbsp butter	▪ Mix all ingredients, except bread crumbs and paprika; place in baking dish.
2 (10 oz) pkgs frozen peas	
6 hard cooked Sunnyfresh Farms Eggs, sliced	▪ Top with crumbs.
1 (10.5 oz) can cream of chicken soup	▪ Drizzle reserved liquid from mushrooms over bread crumbs.
1 cup Steffen's Sour Cream	
¾ cup Steffen's Milk	▪ For more color, sprinkle dash of paprika on top.
1 tsp minced onion	
3 tbsp chopped pimentos	▪ Bake in 375 degree oven for 20 minutes, or until casserole is bubbly.
1 cup soft bread crumbs	
dash paprika (optional)	▪ Serves 6.

availability of wood scraps from the furniture-making trade of the era, almost certainly bred the development of the Dala horse. Initially, the horses were plain wooden toys. In the mid-1800's bright trappings, including the flower-patterned saddle of today, were added to the horses. The saddle's designs are derived from the biblical story in which Jonah sat outside the city of Ninevah and the Lord caused a gourd vine to grow beside him to protect him from the desert sun.

Dala horses gained international popularity when they were chosen by the National Crafts Union for Swedish display at the Paris Exposition in the mid-nineteenth century. They soon became symbols for Swedish handcrafts.

Bethany College is the focal point of intellectual and aesthetic experiences in Lindsborg. The institution's premiere event is the internationally renowned Messiah Festival of Music & Art, held on Palm Sunday and Easter Sunday. The festival has been an annual occurrence since 1882.

The Birger Sandzen Memorial Gallery, also on the college campus, is a tribute to one of America's most prolific and notable artists. Sandzen, a native Swede, arrived in Lindsborg at the age of 23, and never left.

Lindsborg was founded by a group of immigrants who left Sweden in 1868 to make a new home in America's heartland. These settlers were pioneers in cooperative farming and their story is told in the McPherson County Museum at Riverside Park. The building is attached to the Smoky Valley Roller Mill, which has been restored.

Across Mill Street is a complex of historical buildings, including the Swedish pavilion from the 1904 World's Fair in St. Louis. The building was designed and built in Sweden and reassembled at the fair. It was personally dedicated by Carl Gustaf XVI, King of Sweden, during the American Bicentennial.

A huge Swedish-style maypole stands in front of the pavilion. Circles on the pole's crossarm represent friendship. A heart symbolizes love.

The maypole plays a prominent role in Midsommardag, which, next to Christmas, is Sweden's most joyful holiday. After long winter nights, the

Vegetable Casserole

1 (10 oz) pkg frozen broccoli

1 (10 oz) pkg frozen cauliflower

1 cup chopped Bismarck Gardens Carrots

1 (4.5 oz) can button mushrooms

pimento cheese slices, cut into strips

White Sauce:

4 tbsp all-purpose flour

4 tbsp butter

2 cups Steffen's Milk

½ tsp dry mustard

2 tsp Ken's Blend Chili Seasoning

½ tsp Carey Salt

½ tsp pepper

- Partially cook broccoli, cauliflower and carrots.
- Stir in mushrooms and put in baking dish.
- Stir sauce ingredients together until well blended.
- Pour over vegetables and cover with strips of cheese.
- Heat 10 minutes in 350 degree oven.
- Serves 4.

Take-Along Casserole
"Celebrate! Kansas Food" Contest Winner

36 Pendleton's Fresh Asparagus Spears

1 cup chopped onion

¼ cup Steffen's Butter

6 tbsp W-R Unbleached Flour

3 cups Steffen's Milk

2 tsp Carey Salt

¼ tsp pepper

4 hard cooked eggs, sliced

½ cup shredded Pioneer Cheddar Cheese

½ cup dry cracked wheat bread crumbs

- Cook asparagus spears in boiling salted water 10-20 minutes, until barely tender; drain.
- Sauté onion in butter until tender. Stir in flour.
- Add milk and cook, stirring constantly, until thickened.
- Mix in salt, pepper, eggs and asparagus.
- Turn into 2 qt casserole dish.
- Top with cheese and bread crumbs.
- Bake in 350 degree oven until hot and bubbly, 30 minutes.
- Serves 8.

midnight sun associated with the summer solstice is happily anticipated. In each community or small village, the maypole is raised and the dancing begins in celebration of summer. Arts and crafts, demonstrations, Swedish legends and lore, and special activities for children are also an integral part of Midsommardag.

The annual St. Lucia Festival curiously honors a Sicilian. According to Swedish legend, St. Lucia wore a white robe with a crimson sash and a crown of lighted candles. She brought food and drink to hungry Swedes during a famine in the Middle Ages. She also promised there would be gifts for Christmas even though the impoverished Swedes couldn't afford presents for their children.

One of my favorite bed and breakfast inns is Lindsborg's Swedish Country Inn. Its furniture has been imported from Sweden, or made locally, as have the accessories. Rooms have luxurious beds, with goose down pillows and handstitched piecequilts. Each room has a private bath.

The inn's "typical" Scandinavian buffet, each morning, is more like a feast. Specialty breads, pastries, a variety of cheeses and meats, and anything else that suits food service director Alice Brax's fancy, are served. The aroma that permeates the inn is guaranteed to attract even non-breakfast eaters to the dining room.

Twelve great marsh habitats once existed in Kansas, now, there are only three. Although all of them are critical waterfowl habitats, Cheyenne Bottoms, near Great Bend, enjoys a special status as the most important ecosystem in the state.

Elliptical-shaped, the "Bottoms" are approximately six miles long and ten miles wide. Nearly twenty-thousand acres are administered by the Kansas Department of Wildlife and Parks as a wildlife management area. The refuge is a critical habitat for endangered species including the whooping crane, least tern, peregrine falcon and the bald eagle. The latter roosts there during winter months.

DESSERTS

The namesake of The Sunflower State

The International Shorebird Survey has rated Cheyenne Bottoms the top shorebird staging area in the forty-eight contiguous states during migration. Its heartland location midway between the nesting and wintering grounds attracts hundreds of varieties of waterfowl and shorebirds. Some fourteen million birds, or nearly half of the population flying northward, stop there.

On any given day a birdwatcher, camera buff, or gawker will be intrigued by the variety of birds and animals at Cheyenne Bottoms. As I drove down the gravel road to one of the pools, deer bounded in front of me. Huge flocks of ducks, sprinkled with heron, geese and other birds, went about their business oblivious to my presence.

The reception was the same one I had gotten at Quivira National Wildlife Refuge earlier in the day. There, pheasants felt comfortable in my presence. The deer looked up with curiosity but didn't dart.

Although not as well known as Cheyenne Bottoms the 21,820-acre Quivira habitat shares its important role in wildlife conservation. Fish, waterfowl, quail, squirrel, rabbits and doves are among its inhabitants.

The Quivira refuge is located thirteen miles northeast of the community of Stafford.

Fort Larned was the principal guardian of Santa Fe Trail commerce in the 1860's. Several campaigns against the Indians were launched from there. In one such campaign, Custer actually came out a winner. He and his Seventh Cavalry thrust south from the post, into Indian Territory, and defeated Black Kettle's Cheyennes at the Battle of Washita in 1868.

Ironically, Fort Larned's last important function was to help end the usefulness of the trail it had so long protected. In the 1870's, as the railroad pushed west, the fort provided protection for construction workers. It was abandoned in July 1878.

The National Park Service acquired Fort Larned in 1964 and has

Golden Apple Pie

½ cup W-R All-Purpose Flour

⅓ cup sugar

⅓ cup firmly packed brown sugar

½ tsp cinnamon

5 tbsp butter

5-6 cups peeled, thinly sliced King's Orchard Cooking Apples

1 tbsp lemon juice

1½ cups shredded Alma Cheddar Cheese

4 tsp W-R All-Purpose Flour

¼ tsp nutmeg

1 unbaked deep dish 9" pastry shell

Jackson Ice Cream

- Combine flour, sugars and cinnamon; cut in butter. Set aside.
- To prepare filling, toss apples with lemon juice.
- Mix together cheese, flour and nutmeg; toss with apples.
- Arrange apples in pie crust; sprinkle with topping.
- Bake 45-50 minutes in 375 degree oven.
- Top with scoops of ice cream.
- Serves 6-8.

Kansas Kids' Cake
"Celebrate! Kansas Food" Contest Winner

½ cup Steffen's Butter

¼ cup peanut butter

¾ cup Sperry Apiaries Honey

2 Sunnyfresh Farms Eggs

1 tsp vanilla extract

1 cup all-purpose flour

1 cup Old Dutch Mill Whole Wheat Flour

¾ tsp baking soda

1½ tsp baking powder

½ tsp Carey Salt

¾ cup Steffen's Buttermilk

Topping:

½ cup peanut butter

⅔ cup sugar

2 tbsp all-purpose flour

1 cup semi-sweet chocolate pieces

- Cream butter, peanut butter and honey.
- Add eggs and vanilla; mix well.
- Sift dry ingredients; add to mixture, alternating with the buttermilk.
- Pour into greased and floured 9" x 13" pan.
- Mix topping ingredients and crumble over cake.
- Bake in 350 degree oven for 25-30 minutes.
- Serves 10-12.

Cherry Pecan Cake

¾ cup chopped pecans
½ cup butter
2¼ cups W-R All-Purpose Flour
¾ cup sugar
½ cup firmly packed brown sugar
3 tsp baking powder
1 tsp Carey Salt
1 cup milk
1 tsp vanilla extract
2 eggs
1 (21 oz) can cherry pie filling

Frosting:

1 (3 oz) box cherry gelatin
1 (16 oz) ctn whipped topping
pecan halves to garnish

- Grease and flour 2, 8″ or 9″ round cake pans.
- In medium saucepan over low heat, brown pecans and butter until light golden brown, stirring constantly.
- In large bowl, combine flour, sugars, baking powder, salt, milk, vanilla and eggs with browned pecans; beat 2 minutes at medium speed.
- Pour into prepared pans. Bake in 350 degree oven for 25-30 minutes, until toothpick inserted in center comes out clean.
- Cool in pans 5 minutes; invert onto cooling racks to cool completely.
- Fold small amount of dry cherry gelatin into whipped topping.
- Increase amount of gelatin added until desired color is achieved.
- Spread a rim of the frosting mixture about 1″ wide around top edges of each layer.
- Spread cherry pie filling in center of each layer.
- Stack the 2 layers together on serving plate; spread remaining frosting around sides of cake.
- Chill until serving time.
- Decorate top of cake with pecan halves.
- Serves 12.

Apples 'N Honey Nut Tart
"Celebrate! Kansas Food" Contest Winner

Crust:

1¼ cups W-R All Purpose Flour

⅓ cup Kretschmer Wheat Germ

⅓ cup brown sugar

½ tsp Carey Salt

½ tsp grated orange peel

½ cup well chilled Steffen's Butter, cut into pieces

1 egg, beaten

Tart:

1 cup coarsely chopped Carden Pecans

⅓ cup golden raisins

6 tbsp Rainbow Honey Farm Honey

2 tbsp melted Steffen's Butter

¼ tsp grated orange peel

½ tsp cinnamon

4 cups Champlin's Orchard Apple, peeled and cut into ¼" thick slices

⅓ cup orange marmalade

Honey Cream:

⅔ cup whipping cream

2 tbsp Rainbow Honey Farm Honey

- Combine first 5 ingredients.
- Cut in butter and egg with pastry blender until mixture is crumbly.
- Press onto bottom and up sides of 9" x 1" tart pan with a removable bottom.
- Place tart shell in freezer until very firm, about 30 minutes.
- Place pecans and raisins in bottom of chilled crust.
- Combine honey, butter, orange peel, cinnamon and apple slices, mixing to coat apple slices.
- Arrange apple slices in circular pattern on top of pecans and raisins in tart shell; drizzle with honey-butter mixture.
- Bake 50-55 minutes, or until apples are tender.
- Heat marmalade until warm; brush over apples; cool.
- Remove sides of pan.
- Whip cream to soft peaks.
- Add honey and beat until stiff peaks form.
- Serve with tart.
- Makes 8-10 servings.

restored the National Historic Site. Nine buildings form a rectangle around a huge parade ground whose centerpiece is a one hundred-foot flagstaff. Outside the perimeter, to the east, is the blockhouse. Not needed for defense, it served primarily as a guardhouse.

Visitors can take self-guided tours through the Fort Larned site and , occasionally, witness living history demonstrations.

The nearby Santa Fe Trail Center provides additional insight on historical aspects of the fort, trail, and the people of the bygone era.

Greensburg, Kansas, is proud of its big well. After all, it's the largest hand-dug well in the world.

The Santa Fe Railroad needed a dependable source of water for their steam locomotives, and for the people of the area. In 1887 they organized the dig.

Construction was a masterpiece of pioneer engineering. Crews of ten to fifteen farmers, cowboys and other locals—working for fifty cents to a dollar a day—took up picks and spades. Other crews quarried the native stone and hauled it to the site for casing the big hole.

The casing was built on a circular platform supported by jackscrews. As the well deepened, the platform was lowered into the well by turning the screws. The well remained shored and the masons were able to work at ground level.

Water was reached at a depth of one hundred nine feet.

The well is thirty-two feet in diameter and served as the city's water supply until 1932. In 1939, it was covered and opened as a tourist attraction. Since then, more than three million people have visited the site.

There's no charge to look in the well, but if you want to go to the bottom it will cost you a buck. I don't recommend it for couch potatoes or persons not used to exerting themselves. The one hundred five steps are easier to go down than climb up.

The building adjacent to the well is the Greensburg Chamber of

Kansas Apple Cake

¼ cup butter

⅔ cup Elm Creek Honey

1 egg

1 tsp vanilla extract

1 cup The Granary Whole Wheat Flour

1 tsp baking soda

1½ tsp cinnamon

½ tsp nutmeg

¼ cup Kretschmer Wheat Germ

2 cups (about 5 medium) finely diced, unpared Champlin's Orchard Apples

½ cup chopped pecans

whipped cream or ice cream (optional)

- Cream butter; gradually add honey and beat until fluffy.
- Add egg and vanilla; beat thoroughly.
- In separate bowl, combine flour, baking soda, spices and wheat germ.
- Add apples and nuts.
- Stir flour mixture into honey mixture until well blended.
- Spread batter evenly in a greased 8" or 9" square baking pan.
- Bake in 350 degree oven 40-50 minutes, or until cake tests done.
- Cut into squares.
- If desired, top with whipped cream or ice cream.
- Serves 6-8.

Wheat Nub Chocolate Chip Cake

1¾ cups boiling water

1 cup The Kansas Wheat House Wheat Nubs, cracked

1 cup brown sugar

1 cup sugar

½ cup butter

2 eggs

1¾ cups Lormak Farms Mills Whole Wheat Flour

1 tsp baking soda

½ tsp salt

1 tbsp cocoa

1 (6 oz) pkg chocolate chips

- Pour boiling water over cracked wheat nubs; let stand for 10 minutes.
- Add sugars and butter; stir until melted.
- Add eggs and mix.
- Add dry ingredients and chocolates, reserving some chocolate chips to sprinkle on top.
- Pour into greased 9" x 13" pan.
- Sprinkle chocolate chips on top.
- Bake in 350 degree oven for 40 minutes.
- Serves 10-12.

Commerce. It has assorted curios and a visitor from outer space—a Pallasite Meteorite that is half iron and half stone. The meteorite is the largest of its kind yet discovered.

I n October, 1867, fifteen thousand hostile Indians of Great Plains tribes met with representatives of the United States Government at the confluence of Medicine River and Elm Creek, near the present city of Medicine Lodge. It was the largest, most important, and danger-ridden Indian peace council ever held.

Every three years the people of Medicine Lodge and vicinity reenact the great historical events which led up to the confrontation, and the council itself. A cast of two thousand performs in a natural four hundred-acre red rock amphitheatre.

Several times, from the hills surrounding the huge outdoor stage, I've witnessed the Medicine Lodge Peace Treaty Pageant. Scene after spectacular scene unfolded before my eyes as history was relived in the spirit of the prairie and the ancient ceremonials of the Apaches, Kiowas, Arapahoes, Comanches and Cheyenne.

Each pageant performance traces the adventures of Coronado in the Land of Quivira and the exploits of Lewis and Clark, Zebulon Pike, Jim Bridger, Kit Carson and the Pony Express. There is also a dramatic wagon train scene, Indian attack, rescue by the United States Cavalry, and signing of the Peace Treaty of Medicine Lodge.

In past years the pageant has been chosen by the American Bus Association in its annual listings of the top one hundred events in North America.

Medicine Lodge is located in one of the most scenic areas of Kansas, the Gypsum Hills. The region exhibits a butte-mesa-pyramid topography developed largely in predominately red sandstones, siltstones, and shales. White gypsum caps the rims of the dark cedar tree canyons, adding to the scenic grandeur of the hills. Sparse vegetation on the slopes

Amaranth Chocolate Cake

½ cup Cheyenne Gap® Amaranth Flour

1¾ cups flour

2 cups sugar

½ tsp salt

½ cup margarine

3 tbsp cocoa

½ cup vegetable oil

1 cup water

2 Sunnyfresh Farms Eggs

1 tsp cinnamon

1 tsp vanilla extract

½ cup buttermilk

1 tsp baking soda

Frosting:

6 tbsp milk

3 tbsp cocoa

½ cup margarine

1 lb powdered sugar

1 cup chopped walnuts

- Sift together flours, sugar and salt.
- In saucepan, bring to boil margarine, cocoa, oil and water.
- Pour hot mixture over flour and sugar and beat until smooth.
- Add eggs, cinnamon, vanilla and buttermilk, to which baking soda has been added.
- Beat thoroughly; pour into 10½″ x 13½″ cake pan. Bake for 20-25 minutes in 350 degree oven.
- To make frosting, mix together all frosting ingredients and bring to boil; add sugar and walnuts.
- Frost cake while warm.
- Serves 10-12.

Honey of a Pecan Praline Chocolate Cake
"Celebrate! Kansas Food" Contest Winner

¼ cup butter

⅓ cup whipping cream

⅓ cup Rainbow Honey Farm Honey

½ cup brown sugar

1½ cups coarsely chopped Carden Pecans, divided

½ cup butter, softened

⅔ cup brown sugar

¾ cup Rainbow Honey Farm Honey

4 eggs

1 tsp Carey Salt

⅓ cup cocoa

½ cup Kretschmer Wheat Germ

1¾ cups HearTland Mill® Unbleached White Flour

⅔ cup milk

3 tsp baking powder

Topping:

1½ cups whipping cream

3 tbsp Rainbow Honey Farm Honey

⅔ cup coarsely chopped Carden Pecans

- Preheat oven to 325 degrees.
- In a small saucepan, combine first 4 ingredients.
- Cook over low heat until butter melts, stirring occasionally.
- Pour into 2, 9″ round cake pans; sprinkle ½ cup pecans evenly over each pan.
- In a large mixing bowl, combine remaining cake ingredients, in order listed.
- Beat 2 minutes at medium speed until well blended.
- Carefully spoon batter over pecan-honey mixture.
- Bake in 325 degree oven for 35-40 minutes, until toothpick inserted in center comes out clean.
- Cool 5 minutes; remove from pans and cool completely.
- In small bowl, beat cream to soft peaks.
- Add honey and beat until stiff peaks form; fold in pecans.
- To assemble cake, place 1 layer, pecan side up, on serving platter.
- Spread half of whipped cream over top.
- Top with second layer, pecan side up and spread with remaining whipped cream.
- Store in refrigerator until ready to serve.
- Serves 12.

Frozen Strawberry Pecan Yogurt

"Celebrate! Kansas Food" Contest Winner

⅔ cup milk

1 env unflavored gelatin

2 Sunnyfresh Farms Eggs, beaten

⅓ cup sugar

1 pt Rees Fruit Farm Strawberries

⅓ cup Stuart Dietz Honey

1 tbsp lemon juice

1 tsp vanilla extract

2 cups Steffen's Plain Yogurt

½ cup chopped Carden Pecans

- Pour milk into small saucepan; sprinkle gelatin over milk to soften.
- Let stand 5 minutes; add eggs and sugar.
- Cook over medium heat until mixture thickens slightly, stirring constantly.
- Bubbles will form around edges.
- Remove from heat; cool to room temperature.
- Puree strawberries in blender.
- Add gelatin mixture, honey, lemon juice and vanilla to strawberries in blender and thoroughly combine.
- Pour mixture into large bowl and fold in yogurt until no white streaks remain.
- Freeze in ice cream freezer or freeze in 9" x 9" pan in freezer, stirring occasionally, for 2 hours.
- Top with pecans before serving.
- Makes 2 qts.

Trifle

1 pound cake or angel food cake

½ cup sherry or fruit-flavored liqueur

1 cup Chautauqua Hills Jam

2 cups fresh Buckets of Berries Strawberries, Raspberries or Blueberries

2 cups fresh peaches or kiwi

2 cups slivered almonds

2 (3.5 oz) pkgs French vanilla pudding mix, prepared

whipped cream, fruit, slivered almonds to garnish

- Slice prepared cake and layer the slices in the bottom of a trifle dish or large serving bowl.
- Sprinkle cake slices with sherry or liqueur, if desired.
- On top of cake slices, spread jam.
- Layer fresh fruit, a layer of slivered almonds and a layer of pudding.
- Repeat layers, beginning with sliced cake.
- Top with whipped cream, fruit and almonds for garnish.
- Serves 15-20.

Baker University, Baldwin

Crunchy Ice Cream Dessert

1¼ cups Sun Country Granola
¼ cup W-R All-Purpose Flour
¼ cup Kretschmer Wheat Germ
⅛ tsp Carey Salt
⅓ cup brown sugar
½ cup chopped Carden Pecans
¼ cup Steffen's Butter
1 qt Steffen's Butter Pecan Ice Cream,
softened

- Place granola in large mixing bowl.
- Break up large pieces with a wooden spoon.
- Measure ½ cup and reserve for topping.
- Add flour, wheat germ, salt, brown sugar and pecans to granola in bowl.
- Melt butter and add to dry ingredients; mix well.
- Press into buttered 8″ x 8″ baking dish.
- Spread softened ice cream over crust.
- Sprinkle with reserved ½ cup granola; freeze.
- Remove from freezer 5-10 minutes before serving for easier cutting.
- Serves 9.

Jam Cake

½ cup butter, softened
1½ cups sugar
3 Sunnyfresh Farms Eggs
2¼ cups W-R All-Purpose Flour
1 tsp allspice
1 tsp cinnamon
1 tsp nutmeg
½ tsp salt
1 tsp baking powder
½ tsp baking soda
1 cup Aunt Vi's Sand Hill Plum Jam
¼ cup sour milk

- Cream butter; add sugar and beat until light and fluffy.
- Add eggs and beat well.
- Mix together dry ingredients and add to first mixture; beat until well mixed.
- Stir in jam and sour milk.
- Blend thoroughly and spread in an 8″ x 4″ loaf pan that has been greased and floured.
- Bake 25 minutes at 350 degrees.

Variation:
- Add 1 cup nuts, 1 cup raisins and 1 tbsp rum.

permits the colorful rock and shale formations to dominate the scene.

A major "Gyp" Hills activity is an annual weekend trail ride held each May. It has proven to be one of the most colorful, entertaining and exciting outdoor recreation events in the state.

Approximately seven hundred fifty riders on horseback and tractor drawn wagon spread out to roam land once the domain of the five Great Plains Indian tribes who participated in the treaty signing. This same land was also once a part of the Comanche Cattle Pool, the largest cattle ranch in Kansas history.

Medicine Lodge's most famous resident was an ardent foe of alcohol. Her name was Carry A. Nation.

Carry spent most of her early life in Missouri and Texas. She married a dashing young Civil War surgeon of the Union forces, Dr. Charles Gloyd, but their relationship was a stormy one. He was an alcoholic and, to use her phrase, "he filled a drunkard's grave."

Her second marriage, to David Nation, was much happier. He was a lawyer, editor and an ordained minister in the Christian Church.

In 1889, the Nations bought a home in the city of Medicine Lodge. Carry lived in the house for thirteen years. It was from this residence, in 1900, that she began her violent crusade against intoxicants. Carry made her first raid in the nearby town of Kiowa, wielding a hatchet and smashing saloons. From then, until her death, she fought the use of alcohol not only with the blade, but on the stage and chautauqua platform in nearly every state.

Her home is now maintained by the City of Medicine Lodge and is open to visitors.

Susanna Madora Salter, who lived in Argonia to the east, also favored prohibition. She became the first woman mayor in the United States, in 1887, as the result of a joke that backfired.

Salter was a young mother of two and a local temperance leader.

Almond Raspberry Torte

2 eggs, separated
1½ cups whipping cream
1 cup sugar
½ tsp almond extract
1½ cups W-R All-Purpose Flour
1½ tsp baking powder
½ tsp Carey Salt
1 tbsp powdered sugar
¼ cup Chautauqua Hills Raspberry Jam
2 tbsp sliced almonds

- In small bowl, beat egg whites.
- In another bowl, beat whipping cream and fold into egg whites.
- Combine egg yolks, sugar and extract.
- Combine flour, baking powder and salt; add to egg yolk mixture.
- Fold egg white mixture into flour mixture.
- Spread batter in 2 greased and floured 8″ cake pans and bake in 350 degree oven for 20-30 minutes.
- Cool slightly and remove from pans.
- When cake is cooled completely, slice each layer in half.
- In a small bowl, combine whipping cream and powdered sugar until stiff peaks form.
- To assemble torte, place 1 cake layer on tray. Spread with jam and sprinkle with almonds.
- Spread with ¼ cup whipping cream; repeat with 2 more layers.
- Top last layer with jam and pipe or spoon remaining whipped cream around outer edge and sprinkle with remaining almonds.
- Refrigerate until serving time.
- Serves 8-10.

Several Argonia men, who partook of spirits, secretly drew up an election slate with her at the head. It was an attempt to embarrass her with a low vote.

"I didn't know I was on the ballot until I went to the polls," she later recalled. "I stopped my washing to see what all the fuss was about and found people were campaigning for me."

Salter won by a two-thirds majority and served a one-year term. Her first action, upon taking office, was to direct that Argonia's taverns be closed. After that, her tenure was relatively uneventful with the exception of two arrests ordered by city councilmen who were simply testing ordinances.

Salter's recipe for getting along with her all-male council was simple and effective. "The first thing I did," she emphasized, "was to make them think they were the finest men on earth. Never had any trouble after that."

Dexter (population 366) once envisioned a prosperous future. Natural gas was found near the town in 1903 and word of the discovery spread. A crowd gathered to watch the well fired.

Gas roared from the ground just as expected. To everyone's surprise, though, it wouldn't ignite. All flames brought near it were quickly extinguished.

For several years Dexter's gas was scornfully called "wind gas." Then, research by two University of Kansas professors found that the gas contained helium.

The discovery of helium in natural gas led to a multi-million dollar industry but, unfortunately, not in Dexter. Oh, there was a private company that tapped the local gas for use in the U.S. Navy dirigible program. But it's disappeared, just as the blimps have, and the local well no longer produces.

Whenever I'm in Dexter my sweet tooth controls my actions and I pay

COOKIES & CANDIES

A storm brewing over the prairie

a visit to the Henry family. They've been making delicious candy for generations.

Tom Henry and his wife moved from Massachusetts to Little Rock, Arkansas, decades ago. Mrs. Henry originated a chocolate-peanut-caramel candy bar that her husband sold at his "Better Mouse Trap Candy Store." The name was inspired by a Ralph Waldo Emerson essay in which the writer stated, "if a man makes a better mouse trap the public will beat a path to his door."

Tom's son, Pat Henry, Sr., traveled around the country with his father and followed him in the candy-making trade. In 1956, with the help of his wife, Mildred, and his son, Pat Jr., he opened Henry and Son Candy Co., in Dexter.

Henry's makes between 65,000 and 70,000 pounds of candy each year. Included are over one hundred kinds, ranging from hard candy to soft chocolates. Only the best ingredients are used.

On Sunday afternoons, Pat Sr., and other family members make special candies as visitors watch. Between January and August it's usually stick candy or lollipops. If they have an order to fill, that can vary. From August until Christmas they make decorative Christmas candies.

Candies also are made during the week but no special effort is made, as it is on Sundays, to demonstrate the process to the public.

Do they still make candy bars using Tom's wife's recipe? Yes, but rights to the "Tom Henry" candy bar were sold to another company some time ago. And the name was changed to "Oh Henry!"

The Flint Hills Overland Wagon Train Trip is a unique opportunity to see one of Kansas' most scenic regions the way our forefathers did, on board authentic covered wagons.

Once I set foot on the virgin prairie grasses near Rosalia (east of El Dorado) I felt transported back in time. Real cowboys—like wagon-master John Hogeboom who has ranched there all of his 70-plus years—

Corn Flake-Peanut Butter Bars

⅔ cup sugar

⅓ cup light corn syrup

⅓ cup Golden Mill Sorghum

1½ cups chunky peanut butter

½ tsp vanilla extract

¼ tsp butter flavoring

3 cups corn flake cereal

4 (1 oz) squares semi-sweet baking chocolate

- Combine sugar, corn syrup and sorghum in saucepan; slowly bring to a boil, stirring constantly.
- Remove from heat; stir in peanut butter, vanilla and butter flavoring.
- Pour over cereal in a bowl and mix well, being careful to avoid excessive crushing.
- Press into greased 9″ square pan.
- Melt chocolate in glass bowl in microwave, or in saucepan over very low heat, stirring constantly.
- Spread over cereal mixture in pan.
- Let stand until chocolate is firm.
- Cut into 2″ x 1″ bars.
- Makes 36 bars.

Kansas Wheat House Deli Bars

1 cup butter

⅓ cup cocoa

2 cups sugar

1½ cups Kansas Wheat House Flour

4 eggs

1 tsp vanilla extract

1 cup coconut

1 cup Kansas Wheat House S'Wheat Wheat Nubs

1 (13 oz) jar marshmallow cream

1 (16 oz) can chocolate frosting

- Melt butter and cocoa in saucepan.
- Mix sugar and flour together.
- Add melted butter and cocoa to flour mixture.
- Stir in eggs and vanilla.
- Add coconut and wheat nubs.
- Spread on large, greased and floured cookie sheet.
- Bake 20-25 minutes in 350 degree oven.
- While still hot, spread with marshmallow cream.
- Cool and spread with chocolate frosting.
- Makes 40 bars.

round up their fellow "pioneers," Saturday morning, and head prairie schooners out over bumpy terrain. Until Sunday afternoon, civilization as we know it is a thing of the past.

Our camp was set up under a cloudless Kansas sky. Stars twinkled overhead. A blazing campfire made the setting perfect for John to regale us with stories of the old west, then end the evening with a poem he wrote to his wife when they were courting years ago.

The more adventuresome pioneers slept in bedrolls on the ground. Others bunked in the wagons. A few, believing the outdoors experience should end at bedtime, were taken to a motel.

The smell of smoke from a reawakened wood fire, the aroma of coffee brewing, and crisp morning air, made getting up easy. After a hearty breakfast of biscuits and gravy, and eggs and bacon, the horses were hitched to the wagons and we were on our way.

If you've ever wondered why real pioneers spent much of their time walking alongside the covered wagons instead of in them, the wagonmaster provides the answer.

"It wasn't only to lighten the load for the animals," John said, "them boards is hard, pardner!"

Mennonites who settled in Kansas brought with them seeds of Turkey Red Wheat, a hard winter variety much suited to the Kansas prairie. With it, the state became the "Bread Basket of the World."

A large concentration of the religious sect is in South Central Kansas. Hillsboro, Newton, Hesston, Hutchinson, Goessel and other communities have rich Mennonite histories.

The Pioneer Adobe House-Museum in Hillsboro features an original dwelling, and an attached barn, built by Mennonite settlers of the 1870's. A self-conducted tour of original village and other points of historic interest begins there.

The annual spring Mennonite Relief Sale in Hutchinson is the best

Mrs. Eisenhower's Recipe For Uncooked Fudge

Dwight D. Eisenhower Library

4 (1 oz) squares semi-sweet
baking chocolate

4 tbsp butter

1 Sunnyfresh Farms Egg

1 tsp vanilla extract

2 tbsp heavy cream

3½ cups powdered sugar

1 cup chopped Carden Pecans

- Swirl chocolate and butter together over hot water.
- Combine egg, vanilla, cream and sugar.
- Add to chocolate mixture; knead in pecans.
- Turn onto greased platter and chill several hours in the refrigerator before cutting.
- Makes 30-36 squares.

Honey Chippers

½ cup Sperry's Apiaries Honey

½ cup butter

1 egg

1¼ cups W-R All-Purpose Flour, sifted

½ tsp baking soda

½ tsp Carey Salt

½ tsp vanilla extract

1 cup chocolate chips

½ cup chopped Carden Pecans

- Cream honey and butter together.
- Add egg and beat well.
- Sift together dry ingredients; add to creamed mixture; blend well.
- Add vanilla, chocolate chips and pecans.
- Drop by teaspoonfuls onto cookie sheet.
- Bake in 350 degree oven for 12-15 minutes.
- Makes 24 cookies.

place to see this industrious group in action. Traditional Mennonite crafts are shown and sold, delicious food is served, and many of the handmade quilts up for auction bring in thousands of dollars a piece.

The Mennonite Heritage Museum is located in Goessel. It preserves artifacts from early households, farms, schools, churches and the community hospital. It tells the story of the families who left Russia for religious freedom and chose Kansas for their new home.

The museum complex consists of six buildings, including the Immigrant House and the Turkey Red Wheat Palace, as well as historic buildings that were moved to the grounds for preservation and restoration.

The Mennonite Immigrant House is a replica of those shelters built by the Santa Fe Railroad to temporarily house the immigrants. It has forty showcases displaying artifacts, pictures, books, clothing, furniture, household goods and many other things belonging to this early era. A portion of the house is also furnished to portray how the Mennonites lived in similar structures until their own homes were constructed.

The Turkey Red Wheat Palace is a tribute to farmers who introduced and developed the wheat industry in Kansas. It features a blacksmith shop, farm machinery, hand tools and horse-drawn implements relevant to the late 1800's and early 1900's.

Along with the machinery is the Wheat Bell, constructed at the request of the Smithsonian Institution for America's bicentennial celebration. It is a full-scale replica of the Liberty Bell, made of Turkey Red Wheat.

An annual event at the complex is Country Threshing Days, held the first weekend in August. The festival features wheat threshing, antique gas and steam engines, craft demonstrations, ethnic food and entertainment.

Wichita (population 280,000) is the "Air Capital City." Four internationally known aircraft manufacturers—Beech, Boeing, Cessna

Honey Wheat Nuggets

⅓ cup peanut butter

⅓ cup margarine

½ cup Rainbow Honey Farms Honey

1 egg

1 tsp vanilla extract

⅔ cup The Wheat Bin Stone Ground Whole Wheat Flour

¼ tsp salt

½ tsp baking soda

1 tsp baking powder

½ cup non-fat dry milk

½ cup Kretschmer Wheat Germ

1 cup quick cooking oats

1 cup raisins

½ cup chopped nuts

½ cup coconut

½ cup mini chocolate chips

- Cream peanut butter, margarine and honey.
- Add egg and vanilla; mix well.
- Add flour, salt, soda and baking powder.
- Stir in milk, wheat germ and oats.
- Stir in remaining ingredients separately.
- Drop balls, 1″ in diameter, onto greased cookie sheet.
- Bake 8-10 minutes in 350 degree oven.
- Makes 30 nuggets.

Blackberry Jam Bars

¼ cup plus 3 tbsp Steffen's Butter, softened

½ cup brown sugar

1 cup W-R All-Purpose Flour

¼ tsp baking soda

¼ tsp salt

1 cup quick cooking oats, uncooked

1 cup Chautauqua Hills Blackberry Jam

- Cream butter and sugar.
- Combine flour, soda and salt; add to creamed mixture.
- Stir in oats.
- Press half of the mixture into a lightly greased 8″ square pan.
- Top mixture with jam, spreading to within ¼″ of the edge.
- Press remaining crumb mixture firmly on top.
- Bake in 400 degree oven for 30 minutes.
- Makes 30 bars.

and Learjet—have large plants here. It also is a major flour milling, oil producing, oil refining, and wheat and broomcorn marketing center.

The Miss USA pageant, a preliminary competition to the Miss Universe pageant, is now a regular in the city.

Wichita is exciting, especially during the Wichita River Festival, a ten-day event every May. Its focal point is the Arkansas River (Kansans pronounce it "R-Kansas").

A Sundown Parade highlights opening day activities. It is presided over by Admiral Windwagon Smith. Smith is a legendary character whose ship was a conestoga wagon, complete with mast and rudder. He convinced frontier people that he could bring goods quickly to their prairie community if they would build him a prairie schooner.

The schooner was constructed only to be blown away by one of Kansas' famous gusts of win. Some believe, the legend continues, that the windwagon simply disappeared. Others say it can be seen at sunset on a clear day.

Windwagon Smith's modern-day counterpart is seen often during the festival.

Another festival highlight is the Wichita Symphony's twilight pops concert that concludes with a fireworks display. Additional activities include antique bathtub races, a river run, hot air balloons and tasty food.

There are many family attractions in the Wichita area. Frequently visited is the Sedgwick County Zoo. Special care is taken to present animals in their national environment. The zoo has compatible groupings of animals representing geographic areas of the world and the terrain on which they live—even the trees, shrubs, and grasses, as nearly as possible—are designed to duplicate their natural habitats.

The story of Wichita is preserved at the Wichita-Sedgwick County Historical Museum and at the Old Cowtown Museum, a frontier town of more than thirty authentically furnished buildings in Sim Park.

The historical museum occupies the former city hall, a magnificent example of Romanesque architecture built in 1892. It is one of the finest local interpretive centers of its type. Two outstanding exhibits are the

Walnut-Raisin Bars

1 cup raisins
1 cup water
4 Sunnyfresh Farms Eggs
1 cup brown sugar
¾ cup sugar
1⅓ cups Kansas Sun Whole Wheat Flour
1 cup W-R All-Purpose Flour
2 tsp baking powder
½ tsp salt
1 tbsp vanilla extract
1 cup chopped walnuts
powdered sugar to decorate

- Plump raisins with water in covered container overnight.
- Beat eggs and add all ingredients but nuts and raisins; mix well.
- Add nuts and plumped, drained raisins.
- Pour on 15½" x 10½" x 1" greased jelly roll pan.
- Bake in 350 degree oven for 30 minutes, or until done.
- Cut into bars; dust with powdered sugar.
- Makes 40-50 bars.

Golden Pumpkin-Wheat Bars

1½ cups brown sugar
½ cup shortening
1 cup canned pumpkin
1 egg
1 tsp vanilla extract
½ cup water
1 tsp nutmeg
1 tsp cinnamon
1 tsp salt
1 tsp baking powder
1 tsp baking soda
2½ cups The Granary Whole Wheat Flour
½ cup chopped Carden Pecans
1 cup raisins

- Blend the first 6 ingredients until smooth and creamy.
- Sift together nutmeg, cinnamon, salt, baking powder, baking soda and flour; stir into pumpkin mixture.
- Stir in pecans and raisins.
- Grease and flour the bottom of a 9" x 13" pan.
- Bake in 375 degree oven for 20 minutes or until done.
- Makes 24 bars.

Victorian house and the locally-made Jones Six automobile.

Cowtown's Exhibits include Wichita's first jail, a one-room school, the 1869 Munger House, and other homes and businesses that represent early settlement and growth. The Empire House Restaurant and Theatre presents melodramas year-round.

A charming celebration of Christmas past and present is an annual happening at the museum after Thanksgiving. *Christmas Through The Windows* features costumed reenactors preparing for an 1870's Yule. Food and fellowship are an important part of the festivities.

Wichita has three other major attractions in or near Sim Park. Botanica, The Wichita Gardens, features fabulous gardens, lush lawns, intimate and secluded wooded areas.

Relatively new, the gardens are like an exotic plant unfolding one petal at a time. There's something new each time I visit.

Among the completed exhibits are an Entry Garden, a Shakespeare Garden, a Terrace Garden, a Chinese Garden and a Reflecting Pool.

Although I've never seen it on my walks at Botanica, some hikers have reportedly sighted a red fox. However, I can always count on seeing a cottontail rabbit or two, squirrels and a variety of birds.

(Note: Bartlett Arboretum, in suburban Belle Plaine, also has outstanding gardens. The twenty-acre tract of trees, shrubs, flowers and grasses are from all over the world.)

The Wichita Art Museum has one of the nation's most extensive collections of American masterpieces by artists such as Mary Cassatt, Charles Russell, Winslow Homer and Edward Hopper. The Murdock Collection of American Art, from the Colonial period to the twentieth century, the Hands On Gallery of touchable art, and the nationally acclaimed traveling exhibitions are other museum highlights.

The museum's River Room is a popular local gathering spot for weekday lunches and Sunday brunch.

The museum at the Mid-America All-Indian Center focuses on American Indian cultures. The landmark statue "Keeper of the Plains," by artist Blackbear Bosin, stands on its grounds at the confluence of the

Pralines

3 cups sugar
½ cup Steffen's Cream
¾ cup Golden Mill Sorghum
¾ cup light corn syrup
¼ tsp salt
1 cup milk
½ cup butter
1 tbsp vanilla extract
2 cups chopped nuts

- Combine first 7 ingredients; cook until soft ball stage (234 degrees on candy thermometer).
- Remove from heat; add vanilla and nuts.
- Stir rapidly until it begins to thicken.
- Before candy begins to sugar, pour or drop from spoon into cupcake liners or in medium-sized circles on a buttered platter.
- Makes 3 doz.

Carob/Chocolate Chip Cookies

1 egg
2½ tbsp melted butter
2 tbsp water
¼ cup honey
1 cup HearTland Mill® Carob Coffeecake Mix
½ cup chocolate chips

- Mix together the first 4 ingredients and add coffeecake mix.
- Fold in chocolate chips.
- Spoon onto lightly greased cookie sheet and bake in 350 degree oven for 10-12 minutes.
- Makes 1-1½ doz cookies.

Chocolate Chip Honeybees

1¾ cups finely crushed graham cracker crumbs
1 (14 oz) can sweetened condensed milk
2 tbsp Yellow Brick Road Honey
2 tbsp orange or apple juice
1 tsp grated orange rind
1 (6 oz) pkg chocolate chips
½ cup chopped nuts

- Combine cracker crumbs with milk, honey, juice and rind; mix.
- Stir in chips and nuts.
- Spread in oiled, 9″ square pan.
- Bake in 350 degree oven for 30 minutes.
- Cut into squares.
- Makes 36 squares.

Big and Little Arkansas rivers.

Downtown museums include the Wichita Omnisphere and Science Center and the Children's Museum of Wichita.

The Omnisphere has spectacular star shows that explore the heavens through planetarium productions. The museum's collection of science exhibits offers hands-on experiences.

"Please touch" is also often heard at the Children's Museum. The exhibits aren't just for kids, either. Grownups like them, too.

The museum takes an innovative approach to education by permitting children and adults to learn by playing and exploring in a dynamic and colorful environment. Exhibits cover a broad spectrum of topics . . . geography, health, art, science and electronics, to name a few. Displays are changed often to provide the most up-to-date learning tools.

In the Media Center, children can play the part of disc jockeys. They are able to go "on-the-air" over radio station KIDS and hear how they sound.

CMN, the Children's Museum Network, allows youngsters to be television news anchors, weather reporters, or sportscasters. Video recordings are made of their presentations and played back to them on the museum's television monitors.

Other intriguing "discoveries" at the museum include: a Shadow Room where visitors can temporarily "freeze" their shadows on a special wall; a balance wheel that rotates by using the weight differences of its riders; a model railroad; and "Wild Side of Kansas" an exhibit of natural history specimens from throughout the state.

A smaller museum, at the Coleman Company, marks the achievements of "The Greatest Name in the Great Outdoors."

W.C. Coleman founded the company at the turn-of-the century. His featured product was a gas pressure lantern.

Coleman was a Kansas-bred farm boy, school teacher and self-taught engineer. He believed that hard working dirt farmers needed a better light than the smoky yellow glow from old-fashioned coal oil lanterns. What he came up with was a bright white flood light twenty times

SNACKS

Amber waves, Reno County

brighter than the light from the average farm lantern of the era.

His invention soon became known as the great farm lantern, although its usefulness came to be recognized all over the world. Missionaries, explorers and big game hunters introduced the light to some of the darkest parts of seven continents. The lantern is known to have lighted ceremonial dances of New Guinea headhunters, gone with Admiral Richard Byrd to the Antarctic, lighted landing strips in the Andes and brightened docks and sidewalk newsstands in New York City.

In his early days as an entrepreneur, Coleman successfully lighted the first football game played at night on a regulation gridiron. The date was October 6, 1905, and the contestants were Cooper College and Fairmount College, now Wichita State University.

Once the lantern became well established, large numbers were used in search and rehabilitation missions following hurricanes, tornadoes, floods, fires and earthquakes.

Despite the lantern's early successes there were many who predicted that rural electrification would cause the gas lanterns to go the way of the buggy whip. Instead, the "great farm lantern" was destined to become the great camp lantern. To date, more than forty-million have been manufactured and sold.

Shoppers in Wichita can find selections comparable to the nation's largest markets but at prices that reflect the city's down-to-earth, midwestern practicality. Among my favorite places to shop is Sheplers, the "World's Largest Western Store." It sells everything from cowboy boots and Stetsons to designer clothing.

As with every major city, Wichita has outstanding places to eat. My personal favorite is the Cafe Chantilly on East Kellogg. I also like the inexpensive steaks, chicken and shrimp served at Doc's Steak House on North Broadway. The Olive Tree restaurant on North Rock Road has family dining and Mediterranean food, and is very "in" with business

Kansas Krazy Krunch

2 qts popped Steiny's Popcorn

1 cup The Pecan Patch Pecans

⅔ cup peanuts

1⅓ cups sugar

1 cup margarine

½ cup light corn syrup

1 tsp vanilla extract

- Mix popcorn and nuts on a large cookie sheet.
- Combine sugar, margarine and syrup in 1½ qt saucepan.
- Bring to boil over medium heat, stirring constantly. Cook, stirring occasionally, for 10 minutes, or until mixture turns light caramel color.
- Remove from heat; stir in vanilla.
- Pour over popcorn and nuts; coat well.
- Spread out to dry. When dry, break apart.
- Store in tightly covered container.
- Makes 2¼ qts.

Oven Caramel Corn

2 cups light brown sugar

1 cup margarine

½ cup Golden Mill Sorghum

½ tsp Carey Salt

1 tsp vanilla extract

½ tsp baking soda

pinch cream of tartar

15-20 cups popped Myers Gourmet Popcorn

2 cups peanuts

- Heat brown sugar, margarine, sorghum and salt over medium heat to boiling.
- Stir in vanilla, baking soda and cream of tartar.
- Stir very well; pour over popped corn and peanuts, in large pan.
- Mix to coat well.
- Transfer to shallow pans; bake in 250 degree oven for 1 hour, stirring every 15 minutes.
- Cool and store in airtight containers.
- Makes 5 qts.

people visiting the city.

The Crown Uptown Dinner Theatre, on East Douglas, is an acclaimed professional dinner theatre. Buffet meals are served prior to an evening of comedy or drama.

The Wichita Greyhound Track is my pick as "winner" of all the Midwest tracks at which I've dined. Its prime rib and catfish are outstanding! Clubhouse reservations are required on race dates.

Kansas' best tasting potato chips, in my opinion, are manufactured by Art and Mary Kyburz, new kids on the block in the snack food industry. From a small plant near Wichita they fry Art's & Mary's Tater Chips, a delicious snack that has grocers making more room on their shelves.

"That's almost an impossibility these days," Art says. "Stores have only so much space to allot for certain types of products and what's available usually goes to the major manufacturers who have the big bucks to pay for it. We don't have the money to compete that way so we've gone to the people, created a demand, and used our popularity to get inside the doors."

At an age when most people are thinking of retirement, the Kyburzes became hucksters on weekends and evenings to introduce Art's & Mary's Tater Chips to Kansans. At home shows, travel shows or anywhere they could work a crowd, the two passed out free samples of their new product from a small booth.

"The first time we used this marketing approach was at a Wichita boat show in the early 1980's," he recalls. "As people went by, we invited them over to try our chips. They liked what they ate and asked where they could buy them. We said, 'you can't, but take this business card to your grocer and tell him you want us.' That's exactly what they did and have been doing since."

The Kyburzes moved to Wichita from Pennsylvania where Art had worked in the snack food industry. The first chips they sold weren't as eagerly accepted by Kansans as the couple thought they would be.

"We almost had to close the doors," Art recalls, "before we discovered people here won't buy the same lard-fried chip that's popular back East.

Zesty Cheese Popcorn

½ cup melted butter

½ cup shredded Alma Cheddar Cheese

⅓ cup crumbled Oakland Pork Bacon

1 tbsp soy sauce

½ tsp onion powder

¼ tsp celery salt

¼ tsp garlic salt

1½ cups unpopped Gary D. Schlaegal's Homegrown Popcorn, popped

- Combine butter, cheese, bacon and seasonings until well blended.
- Spread popcorn in a large roasting pan.
- Pour cheese mixture over popcorn and toss lightly to mix.
- Bake in 250 degree oven for 1 hour, stirring 4-5 times.
- Store in an airtight container.
- Makes 5 qts.

Microwave Sunny Popcorn Snack

10 cups popped Twin Valley Plain Popcorn

¾ cup Kansas Nutworks Sunflower Nuts

½ cup pecans, chopped

¼ cup Jeffries Family Apiary Honey

½ cup packed brown sugar

¼ cup butter

1 tsp vanilla extract

- Place popped corn in buttered 3 qt microwave casserole. Add sunflower nuts and pecans; set aside.
- Combine honey, brown sugar and butter in a 4 cup glass measure.
- Microwave on HIGH, uncovered, 2-3 minutes, or until mixture boils, stirring once.
- Then microwave on HIGH 2 minutes, allowing mixture to boil 2 minutes, stir in vanilla.
- Pour hot mixture over popped corn.
- Using 2 spatulas toss lightly until evenly mixed.
- Microwave on HIGH, uncovered, 4½-5½ minutes, or until lightly toasted, stirring 4-5 times.
- Turn onto baking sheet and allow to cool.
- Makes 12 cups.

"From January through August of 1983, business didn't get better, it got worse. I surveyed customers coming into our outlet, at the front of the plant . . . noting whether they were buying for the first time or were repeat business . . . and discovered very few people had returned," he continues. "Taste and health concerns seemed to be the reasons." A switch to peanut oil was made.

Art contends that Kansans balked at consuming lard because it's animal fat.

"Even people who liked how the lard-cooked chip tasted decided not to buy from us again after reading the ingredients listed on the package," he points out. "No matter that the bacon or sausage they had for breakfast had high levels of cholesterol, lard was a 'no, no.' Peanut oil, though, is cholesterol-free and produces a good-tasting chip. Since we started frying with it our sales have risen steadily."

The Kyburzes say customers get more potatoes for their money in an Art's & Mary's bag than they do in those of most other brands.

"The major manufacturers usually fry their chips faster and in a hotter oil than we do," Art emphasizes. "Thus, they don't have as much shrinkage."

The Kyburzes know they'll never be giants in the potato chip industry, but they have found they can compete by making a quality product.

Mexican Popcorn

2½ qts popped Big Top Popcorn
⅓ cup melted butter
1 tsp Ken's Blend Chili Seasoning
⅓ tsp crushed, dried chilies (optional)

- Toss all ingredients together.
- Makes 2½ qts.

Honey Snack

⅓ cup unpopped Prairie Popcorn,
popped
1 cup The Pecan Patch Pecans
½ cup butter
1 cup brown sugar
¼ cup Rainbow Honey Farm Honey
½ tsp salt
¼ tsp cinnamon
¼ tsp nutmeg
1 tbsp water

- Combine popcorn and pecans.
- Keep warm in 250 degree oven.
- In a 2 qt saucepan, melt butter.
- Stir in brown sugar, honey, salt, cinnamon, nutmeg and water.
- Cook over medium heat until boiling, stirring constantly.
- Boil mixture to hard crack stage (300-310 degrees on a candy thermometer).
- Place popcorn mixture in large bowl.
- Slowly pour honey glaze over popcorn mixture, stirring to coat.
- Spread in a buttered jelly roll pan and return to 250 degree oven for 20 minutes, stirring once after 10 minutes.
- Cool.
- Break into pieces.
- Makes 2½ qts.

BUYER'S GUIDE

Bakery Products

Bakery and Deli of Ah's, Topeka
Being Good To Me Cookie Co.,
    Norcatur
Best Of The Sweet Country, Alta Vista
Betty's Tas-Tee Pies, Kansas City
Cookies By Carolyn, Little River
Dillon Stores, Hutchinson
Earthly Endeavors, Wichita
Frontenac Bakery, Frontenac
Gourmet 500 (Slade Homestead Bread
    & Cookies), Wichita
Helmuth Country Bakery, Hutchinson
Home Town Cafe, Barnes
Homemade Breads By Nancy, Salina
Interstate Brands Corporation (Dolly
    Madison), Emporia
Kathy's Bakery, Overland Park
Kingfisher's Inn, Marion
Mitten Cafe Bakery, Oakley
N & J Pita Bakery, Valley Center
Rainbo Baking Company, Hutchinson
Rainbo Baking Company, Wichita
Richferd's Ent. Inc., Atchison
Seven Sisters Bakery, Holton
Silks Fine Foods, Lawrence
Sophie's Bakery & Coffeehouse,
    Overland Park
The Courtyard Bakery, Lindsborg
The Little Red Hen Bake Shoppe,
    Hutchinson
Troyers Home Pantry, Galva
Vista Franchise, Inc., Manhattan
Willow Pantry, Wichita

Beverages

Applematics Orchard, Jamestown
Balkan Winery, Girard
EVCO Wholesale Coffee, Emporia
Fields Of Fair, St. George
Louisburg Cider Mill, Louisburg
Maple Leaf Orchards, Inc.,
    Baldwin City
Pepsi Cola Bottling of Topeka, Topeka
Rees Fruit Farm, Inc., Topeka
Seven-Up Bottling Co., Topeka
Sunny Cal, Kansas City

Candy/Confections

Bowers' Penny Annies, Lawrence

Heartland Food Products, Inc., Lenexa
Henry's Candies, Dexter
Kaw Valley Farms, Manhattan
Lik'm Lollipops, Hutchinson
Mrs. Burden's Gourmet Candy
    Company (DouxBonte), Sedan
Phillips Confections, Lawrence
Plaza Popcorn And Fudge Co., Merriam
Sifers Valomilk Candy Cups, Merriam
Squareshooter Candy Co., Inc. (Norton,
    Ann Raskas), Edwardsville
The Kansas Wheat House, Inc. (Minute
    Wheat, Wheat Nub, S'Wheat),
    Cimarron
Warfel's Homemades, Alma
Westward Industries, Inc. (Skadadles,
    Salad Expression), Wichita

Dairy Products

Alma Cheese, Alma
Bern Meat Plant, Bern
Duis Meat Processing, Inc. (Duis
    Delights), Concordia
Jackson Ice Cream Co., Inc. (Dillon's),
    Hutchinson
Mid America Dairymen, Inc. (Bit O'
    Gold), Wamego
Mid-America Dairymen, Inc., Sabetha
Ozark Salad Company (R. B. Rice,
    Priddy's), Baxter Springs
Pioneer Cheese Company, Inc.,
    Moundridge
Steffen Dairy Foods Co., Inc.
    (Steffen's), Wichita

Egg and Egg Products

Cal-Maine Foods, Inc. (Sunnyfresh
    Farms), Buhler
Wetta Egg Farm, Inc. (Wat-A-Egg),
    Andale

Flour

American White Wheat Producers,
    Atchison
Cheyenne Gap Amaranth, Luray
Daylight Donuts of Winfield, Winfield
Dillon Stores, Hutchinson
Groth Farms, Inc., Satanta
Heartland Mill, Inc., Marienthal
Lormak Farms Mills, Concordia

Old Dutch Mill, Wamego
Stafford County Flour Mills Company,
  Hudson
The Granary, Downs
The Wall-Rogalsky Milling Co. (W-R),
  McPherson
The Western Star Mill Company, Salina
The Wheat Bin, Inc. (The Wheat Bin),
  Halstead

Cereals/Staples/Mixes

C P I Corporation ("Sunnywheat,"
  Tastycrust), Wichita
Central Soyfoods, Lawrence
Dawn's, Inc. (Best in the West), Ingalls
Heartland Food Products, Inc., Lenexa
Heartland Mill, Inc., Marienthal
Heartland Mixes, Marion
Irsik & Doll Feed Services, Inc.,
  Cimarron
Kansas Fisheries (Prairie King),
  Wichita
Kansas Restaurant Association (Kansas
  Sunflower Honey Wheat Bread,
  "Sunnywheat"), Wichita
Lormak Farms Mills, Concordia
McKinney's Indian Fry Bread, Mayetta
Old Dutch Mill, Wamego
Pines International, Inc., Lawrence
Pony Express Ranch, Marysville
Quaker Oats Company (Kretschner,
  Sun Country), Wichita
Rabbit Creek Products, Louisburg
Sigco Sun Products, Breckenridge
The Amaran Corporation, Oberlin
The Basket Place, Lawrence
The Downstairs, Mission
The Granary, Downs
The Kansas Soup Lady, Wamego
The Wall-Rogalsky Milling Co. (W-R),
  McPherson
The Wheat Bin, Inc., Halstead
Windmill Inn, Inc., Seneca
Westward Industries, Inc. (Skadadles,
  Salad Expression),Wichita

Gift Boxes/Baskets

Birk's Gift Gallery, Wamego
Carousel Gift Shop, Topeka
Chautauqua Hills Jelly Co., Sedan
The Country Cupboard, Leavenworth
Creative Kansas Gift Baskets, Topeka
Duis Meat Processing, Inc., Concordia

Emerald Gardens, Williamsburg
Happy Shanty Gift & Frame Shop,
  Kansas City
The Hay Market (The Best of Kansas),
  Wichita
Heartland Gift Baskets, Garden City
Kansas Favorites, Baldwin City
Kansas Gift Baskets, Belleville
Kansas Gold, Hays
Kansas Kountry Baskets, Topeka
Kansas Treasures, Marquette
The Kansas Wheat House, Inc. (Minute
  Wheat, Wheat Nub, S'Wheat),
  Cimarron
Mabel's Kitchen, Overland Park
Natural Gifts (Flint Hills Gold),
  Hartford
Rainbow Honey Farm, Concordia
The Wheat Bin, Inc., Halstead

Honey

B & B Apiary, Lincoln
Brubaker Apiaries (Sunflower State
  Brand), Salina
Don Schmidt Honey, Greensburg
E. W. Holden, Topeka
Emerald Gardens, Williamsburg
Floyd's Fruits and Vegetables, Eudora
Fowler Honey Farms, Wichita
Friesen Honey Farm, McPherson
Green Valley Farm, Leavenworth
Gross Orchard, Wilson
H & H Honey Company, Sterling
Hadorn's Pure Clover Honey,
  Marysville
Hamel Honey Farms, Hays
Hawley Honey Co. (Sweetheart Honey),
  Iola
High Plains Honey, Ensign
Honey Tree Farm, Salina
Hosack's Honey, Eureka
J & B Apiaries, Eskridge
Jeffries Family Apiary, Lawrence
Kansas City Stinger's, Kansas City
Larry Keeler, Tonganoxie
Levin Honey Farm, Versailles
Local Honey, Kansas City
M & G Honey Farms, Bushton
Marteney's Pastel Hives, Wamego
McBurney Apiary, Quinter
Mike's Family Honey Farm, McLouth
Mr. K's Apiary, Frankfort
Murphy's Honey Farm, Kansas City

Natural Gifts, Hartford
Noel's Honey, Kansas City
Pearson Honey Farm, Ingalls
Pickett's Gardens & Greenhouse,
  Burlingame
Rainbow Honey Farm, Concordia
Rees Fruit Farm, Inc., Topeka
Smokey Hill Bee Farm, Ellsworth
Speckman Honey, Shawnee
Sperry Apiaries (Sperry Apiaries),
  Pittsburg
Stevens Apiaries (Yellow Brick Road),
  Pratt
Stuart Dietz Honey Farms, Topeka
Twin Elm Apiaries, Belle Plaine
Ungerer Apiaries (Elm Creek),
  Marysville
West Glen Honey Products, Topeka
Young's Honey, Kansas City

Jams, Jellies, Preserves

Best Of The Sweet Country, Alta Vista
Briarwood Farms, Ltd., Alma
Chautauqua Hills Jelly Co. (Chautauqua
  Hills), Sedan
Louisburg Cider Mill, Louisburg
Piccadilly Market, Wichita
R & T Jellies, Concordia
Seybert Food Processing, Inc. (Aunt
  Vi's), Meade

Meat Products

Bern Meat Plant, Bern
Dillon Stores, Hutchinson
Ellis County Processing, Hays
Flint Hills Foods, Inc. (Western Brands
  Meats), Wamego
Gerald Blazek Farm, Munden
Hiawatha Locker & Processing,
  Hiawatha
Hoseney's Dressed Beef and Pork,
  Coffeyville
Kansas Export Beef, Inc., Junction City
Kansas Pork Producers Council,
  Manhattan
Kingman Processing, Kingman
Klema Locker Service, Wilson
Klema Quality Meats (Solomon Valley
  Pride), Beloit
Kolklatzers Family Products, Larned
Krehbiel's Kountry Store, Inc.
  (Krehbiel's), McPherson
Linn Locker Plant, Linn

Lone Pine Acres, Inc. (Lone Pine
  Farms), Lecompton
Luthers Smokehouse, LeRoy
Macomber Meat Processing (Hickory
  Point), Winchester
Manhattan Wholesale Meat (Manco),
  Manhattan
Oakland Pork, Miltonvale
Roepke's Processing Plant, Waterville
Schmidt Packing Co., Meade
Shaw's Grocery, Wilson
Smoky Hill Sausage Co., Hays
Smoky River Meats (Duis Delights),
  Salina
Stoffle Meat Co., Topeka
Swift-Eckrich, Inc., Lenexa
Triple "S" Meat Company, Inc. (Nutri-
  Beef), Wichita
Valley Vista Locker, Topeka
Wamego Facility - Flint Hills Foods
  (Das Smokehaus, Nehring Farms),
  Wamego

Processed Meats

Alta Vista Locker, Inc., Alta Vista
Best Of The Sweet Country (Best Of
  The Sweet Country), Alta Vista
Duis Meat Processing, Inc. (Duis
  Delights), Concordia
Ellis County Processing, Hays
Erika's Bratwurst, Woodbine
Fanestil Packing Co., Inc., Emporia
Galey's Meats & Deli (Galey's), Garnett
Heideman Meats, Seneca
Hiawatha Locker & Processing,
  Hiawatha
Kolklatzers Family Products, Larned
Krehbiel's Kountry Store, Inc.
  (Krehbiel's), McPherson
Lone Pine Acres, Inc., Lecompton
Luthers Smokehouse, LeRoy
Macomber Meat Processing,
  Winchester
McGreevy's Mid West Meat Co., Inc.,
  Wichita
Ohse Meat Products, Inc. (Ohse),
  Topeka
Oldham's Farm Sausage, Kansas City
Peabody Sausage House (Grandma's
  Homestyle Mustard), Peabody
Pony Express Ranch (Pony Express
  Ranch Ham), Marysville

Pyle Meat Co., Inc. (Hombre Brand),
  Eudora
Quinter Meat Processors (Castle Rock
  Brand), Quinter
Ricci D's Sausage, Inc., Moundridge
Roepke's Processing Plant, Waterville
Schmidt Packing Co., Meade
Schuetz Locker Co. (Maken-Lite),
  Atchison
Smoky Hill Sausage Co., Hays
Smoky River Meats, Salina
Swift Premium, Lenexa
Valley Vista Locker, Topeka
Wamego Facility—Flint Hills Foods
  (Das Smokehaus, Nehring Farms),
  Wamego

Meat Products—Specialized Items

Best Butcher, Rose Hill
Butterfield's Buffalo Meat, Beloit
Culver Fish Farm (Culver Fish Farm),
  McPherson
Farmer's Fallow Deer, Viola
Heartland Fish Co., Garden City
Hoseney's Dressed Beef and Pork,
  Coffeyville
Meadow Land Spring Trout Farm,
  Morrill
Spring Hill Farm, Winfield
Springhills Fish Farm, Abilene
Thunder Of The Plains Buffalo, Inc.,
  Fowler
Underhill Farms, Moundridge

Nuts

Carden Pecan Co., Chetopa
Kansas Nutworks (Golden Roast, Cajun
  Spice), Wichita
Smoky Valley Grains, Marquette
The Kansas Wheat House, Inc.,
  Cimarron
The Pecan Patch, Wichita
The Soy Bin (Emogene's Soy Goodies),
  Marienthal

Pasta Products

Bauman's Homemade Noodles, Garnett
Dinah's Noodles, Inc. (Dinah's Noodles),
  Clyde
Grandma's Noodles (Grandma's
  Noodles), LaCrosse

Helmuth Country Bakery, Hutchinson
Pasta Concepts, Inc. (Pasta Mills),
  Wichita

Pizza

Gourmet Pizza of Kansas, Inc., Russell
Tony's Pizza Service (Red Baron, Café
  Mexico), Salina

Popcorn

Big Top Popcorn (Big Top Popcorn,
  Kernel C. M. Sweet), Topeka
Emerald Gardens, Williamsburg
Gary D. Schlaegel's Homegrown
  Popcorn, Whiting
Heartland Popcorn, Lenexa
Irvine Popcorn, Topeka
Myers' Gourmet Popcorn, Garden City
Nimtz Farms (Uncle Charlie's Popcorn),
  Wathena
Pioneer Marketing (Corn Crib Popcorn),
  Wichita
Plaza Popcorn and Fudge Co., Merriam
Prairie Popcorn, Alta Vista
Steiny's Homegrown Popcorn, Downs
The Popcorn Exchange (Pop Perfect),
  Garden City
Twin Valley Developmental Services,
  Inc., Greenleaf
Uncle Ozgood's Products, Copeland
Williams Foods, Lenexa
Zarda Popcorn, Overland Park
Zweygardt's Popcorn, St. Francis

Produce

Barbra Britt (Britt's Garden Acres),
  Manhattan
Bauman Farms, Waverly
Bismarck Gardens (Bismarck Gardens),
  Lawrence
Buckets of Berries (Buckets of Berries),
  Baldwin City
Champlin's Orchard (Champlin's
  Orchard), Concordia
Coltrain Vegetables, Neodesha
Country Store, Moundridge
Dan Bourquin Farms (Organic Country
  Table), Colby
David's Herbs, Perry
Dillon Stores, Hutchinson
Emerald Gardens, Williamsburg
Floyd's Fruits and Vegetables, Eudora

G H Farms, Hutchinson
Groh Orchards, Inc. (Valley Pride
    Apples), Wathena
Irvine Popcorn, Topeka
J. C. Meier & Sons, Topeka
King's Orchard, Wichita
Knackstedt's, Inman
Loyd's, Downs
Merritt Horticultural Center,
    Kansas City
Meyer's Garden Spot and Greenhouse,
    Wichita
Moore Orchard, Newton
Ozark Salad Company (R. B. Rice,
    Priddy's), Baxter Springs
Pendleton's Fresh Kaw Valley,
    Lawrence
Pickett's Gardens & Greenhouse,
    Burlingame
Polk's Farm, Burrton
Rees Fruit Farm, Inc., Topeka
Sargeant Strawberry Farm, Wichita
Sat Nam Sprouts, Lawrence
Schultz Farms, Arlington
Sunflower Organic Farm, Edgerton
Tim Oberhelman (Harvest House),
    Edgerton
Toto Cure of Kansas, Inc., Atchison
Turner's Orchard, Kansas City
Twin Rivers Vineyard, Valley Center
Whole Earth Farms, Mt. Hope
Wildwood Flowers, Gifts & Crafts,
    Holton

Barbecue Sauces

Chambers Rollin' Rib Kage Bob-B-Q,
    Emporia
Chef Dan's, Inc., Merriam
Cinda's Smoke Sauce, Valley Center
Flower of the Flames, Inc., Shawnee
    Mission
Hayward's Pit, Inc., Overland Park
Kay-Pat-Al and Company (Bob's-B-Q-
    Sauce), Topeka
Kingsfords Original K Barbecue Sauce,
    Shawnee Mission
Lane's Barbecue, Topeka
P M S Foods, Inc. (Curley's Bar-B-Que
    Sauce, Imagic Bakon Crumbles),
    Hutchinson
The Recipe Exchange (Kansas City's
    Baron of Barbeque), Shawnee Mission
Valley Vista Locker, Topeka

Seasonings/Spices

American Salt Company (Carey),
    Mission
K. C. Rib Doctors, Inc., Shawnee
Kenlo Enterprises (Ken's Original Chili
    Seasonings, Ken's Blend), Wichita
Melanie's Spices, Concordia
Olde Westport Spice & Trading Co.
    (Olde Westport, Trader Bill's),
    Overland Park
Palacky Industries (Prairie Bounty),
    Wichita
Pedro Lopez Co., Inc., Topeka
Williams Foods, Lenexa

Snack Products

Art's Tater Chip Co., Inc. (Art's &
    Mary's), Wichita
Becerros Mexican, Inc., Lawrence
Frito-Lay, Inc. (Lays, Ruffles, Doritos,
    Tostitos, Cheetos, Funyuns, Fritos,
    Crunch, Tators, Santitas), Topeka
Kaw Valley Farms (Crispy Corn),
    Manhattan
La Siesta Foods, Inc. (La Siesta, El
    Toro), Topeka
Pendleton's Fresh Kaw Valley (Blue
    Corn Chips), Lawrence
Spanish Gardens Food Mfg. Co., Inc.,
    Kansas City
Waybo Foods, Inc., Moundridge
White Cloud Grain Company, Inc.
    (Santa Fe), Hiawatha

Miscellaneous

B & R Bierocks, St. Francis
Cafe International Foods (Mama Lupe),
    Topeka
Golden Mill Sorghum, Bartlett
J. B.'s Neat To Eat, Wichita
Lems, Inc., Hutchinson
Markham's Cider Mill Products
    (Sweethot Apple Cider
    Mustard), Tonganoxie
Multi-Business Service Corp. (Zula
    Sauce), Wichita
New Mexico Tortilla Kitchen & Bakery,
    Topeka
Nina Ltd. (Fuego), Lenexa
Toma Products (Toma), Wichita
The Whole Enchilada's, Wichita

INDEX

SAVE 25¢

2 lb. package KWIK MIX

Whole Wheat All Purpose Baking Mix

Limit one package

From **THE WHEAT BIN,** Inc.

R.R. 1, Box 64, Halstead, KS 67056

Retailaer or Grocer: We will pay face value plus 8c handling.
Cash Vaue 1/20 of 1 cent. Expires May 5, 1991

This Coupon Worth

$2.00

on the purchase of a
6 1/2 gallon decorated tin
of flavored popcorn

Myers' Gourmet Popcorn

119 West Grant Avenue
Garden City, Kansas 67846
316-275-5751

SAVE 10¢

2 lb. package Stone Ground

WHOLE WHEAT FLOUR

Limit one package

From **THE WHEAT BIN,** Inc.

R.R. 1, Box 64, Halstead, KS 67056

Retailer or grocer: We will pay you face value, plus 8c handling.
Cash value 1/20 of 1 cent. Expires May 5, 1991.

55¢ OFF
ANY TWO 3.5 OZ.
3 PACK BOXES

TO CONSUMER: Limit one coupon per purchase. Offer not valid in conjunction with any other offer. Reproduction of coupon prohibited.

RETAILER: We will redeem this coupon for face value and in accordance with our redemption policy, and if upon request you submit invoices for the quantity of product for which coupons are redeemed. Cash value 1/100c. For redemption mail to: THE POPCORN EXCHANGE, P.O. Box 538 Garden City, KS 67846

MANUFACTURER'S COUPON   EXPIRES: MAY 5, 1991

SAVE 20¢

5 lb. package Stone Ground

WHOLE WHEAT FLOUR

Limit one package

From **THE WHEAT BIN,** Inc.

R.R. 1, Box 64, Halstead, KS 67062

Retailer or Grocer: We will pay face value plus 8c handling.
Cash Value 1/20 of 1 cent. Expires May 5, 1991.

.⋆ *The* ⋆.

Country Cupboard

Your Source for Kansas Gifts and Gift Baskets
WE SHIP WORLDWIDE
203 Delaware • Leavenworth, KS • 913-682-4522

This coupon good for one FREE
"From The Land of Kansas" food product with
purchase of *"From the Land of Kansas"* food
product of equal or greater value.

SAVE 55¢

when you buy a 2 lb. jar
GOLDEN MILL SORGHUM

TO GROCER:.
For redemption, mail to Golden Mill Sorghum, Rt. 1, Box 29, Bartlett, Kansas 67332. All sales tax must be paid by consumer.

Expiration Date: June 1, 1991.

WHEAT
The Natural Healthy Treat

BUY 2 3oz. Wheat Nubs
GET 1 FREE

The Kansas Wheat House, Inc.
Box 1051
Cimarron, KS 67835
(316) 855-3489

55¢ off
HURRY! EXPIRES APRIL 30, 1991

OhSe
HONEY CURED
OR PIT BRAND HAM

GROCER: Redeem on terms stated for consumer upon purchase indicated. ANY OTHER USE CONSTITUTES FRAUD. For reimbursement of face value plus 8¢ mail to OhSe Foods, Inc., P.O. Box 880792, El Paso, Texas 88588-0792. Failure to produce upon request invoices proving purchase of stock covering coupons may void all coupons submitted. Void if taxed, restricted, prohibited or presented by other than retailers of our products. Cash value 1/100¢ One coupon per purchase. Consumer pays any sales tax

74800 145562

$5 Discount
on
Gift Baskets
Kansas FAVORITES
Regularly Priced $35 or more

===== Order From =====

Cygnet Fashions & Fabrics
713 8th St. • Rt. 3, Box 159
Baldwin City, KS 66006
913-594-3477

We accept Visa, MC & Discover

Expires May 5, 1991

CHEYENNE GAP®
AMARANTH
30¢ OFF
3 lbs. Fine Amaranth Flour
or
25¢ OFF
Whole Grain To Grind

Arris A. Sigle
HC 1, Box 46
Luray, KS 67649

EXPIRES 5/5/91

TOUCH BY A RAINBOW
Great Cooking Land of Kansas

- A $19.95 value offered at a special discount of $16.95
- Kansas manufacturers coupons inside the book are valued over $30

Please send ___ copy (copies) of **TOUCH BY A RAINBOW Great Cooking From The Land Of Kansas** @ $16.95/copy, plus $2.50 freight to: (Make check or money order out to Leisure Time Publishing, 9029 Directors Row, Dallas, TX. 75247)

Name: _____

Address: _____

City/State/Zip:_____ Phone:_____

TOUCH BY A RAINBOW
Great Cooking Land of Kansas

- A $19.95 value offered at a special discount of $16.95
- Kansas manufacturers coupons inside the book are valued over $30

Please send ___ copy (copies) of **TOUCH BY A RAINBOW Great Cooking From The Land Of Kansas** @ $16.95/copy, plus $2.50 freight to: (Make check or money order out to Leisure Time Publishing, 9029 Directors Row, Dallas, TX. 75247)

Name: _____

Address: _____

City/State/Zip:_____ Phone:_____

TOUCH BY A RAINBOW
Great Cooking Land of Kansas

- A $19.95 value offered at a special discount of $16.95
- Kansas manufacturers coupons inside the book are valued over $30

Please send ___ copy (copies) of **TOUCH BY A RAINBOW Great Cooking From The Land Of Kansas** @ $16.95/copy, plus $2.50 freight to: (Make check or money order out to Leisure Time Publishing, 9029 Directors Row, Dallas, TX. 75247)

Name: _____

Address: _____

City/State/Zip:_____ Phone:_____

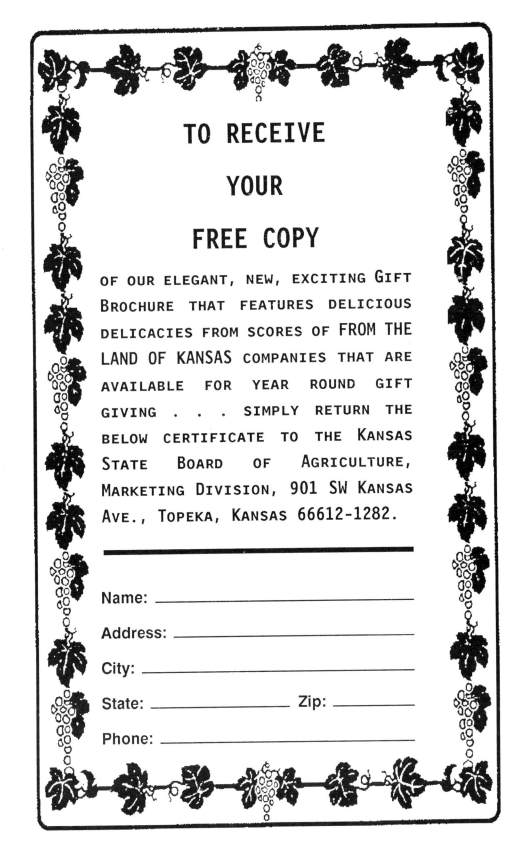

TO RECEIVE

YOUR

FREE COPY

OF OUR ELEGANT, NEW, EXCITING GIFT BROCHURE THAT FEATURES DELICIOUS DELICACIES FROM SCORES OF FROM THE LAND OF KANSAS COMPANIES THAT ARE AVAILABLE FOR YEAR ROUND GIFT GIVING . . . SIMPLY RETURN THE BELOW CERTIFICATE TO THE KANSAS STATE BOARD OF AGRICULTURE, MARKETING DIVISION, 901 SW KANSAS AVE., TOPEKA, KANSAS 66612-1282.

Name: _____

Address: _____

City: _____

State: _____ Zip: _____

Phone: _____

FROM THE LAND OF KANSAS is a registered trademark of the Kansas State Board of Agriculture.

The trademark was initiated in 1984 and is available to producers and processors of Kansas foods to increase visibility and sales. Hundreds of products proudly display the FROM THE LAND OF KANSAS trademark.

The trademark program is a full-service marketing effort to develop support, pride and profits among producers, processors, retailers, food services and consumers. More than 300 companies are currently using the trademark to promote their products.

These ongoing and diversified FROM THE LAND OF KANSAS events are available to all Kansas food companies. The campaign includes promotion of trademark products in grocery stores, specialty shops, restaurants and schools, as well as through mail order, trade shows, public service announcements through radio and television, print publications, and special events.

The regulations for using the FROM THE LAND OF KANSAS trademark and application forms are available from the Kansas State Board of Agriculture, Marketing Division, 901 SW Kansas Ave., Topeka, Kansas 66612-1282. If you have any questions, call (913) 296-3737.